THE
NATASHAS

Also by Victor Malarek

Gut Instinct

Merchants of Misery

Haven's Gate

Hey . . . Malarek!

THE NATASHAS

THE NEW GLOBAL SEX TRADE

VICTOR MALAREK

VIKING
CANADA

VIKING CANADA

Penguin Group (Canada), a division of Pearson Penguin Canada Inc.,
10 Alcorn Avenue, Toronto, Ontario M4V 3B2

Penguin Group (U.K.), 80 Strand, London WC2R 0RL, England
Penguin Group (U.S.), 375 Hudson Street, New York, New York 10014, U.S.A.
Penguin Group (Australia) Inc., 250 Camberwell Road, Camberwell, Victoria 3124, Australia
Penguin Group (Ireland), 25 St. Stephen's Green, Dublin 2, Ireland
Penguin Books India (P) Ltd, 11, Community Centre, Panchsheel Park,
New Delhi – 110 017, India
Penguin Group (New Zealand), cnr Rosedale and Airborne Roads, Albany, Auckland 1310,
New Zealand
Penguin Books (South Africa) (Pty) Ltd, 24 Sturdee Avenue, Rosebank 2196, South Africa

Penguin Group, Registered Offices: 80 Strand, London WC2R 0RL, England

First published 2003

1 2 3 4 5 6 7 8 9 10   (FR)

Copyright © Victor Malarek, 2003

Author representation: Westwood Creative Artists
94 Harbord Street, Toronto, Ontario M5S 1G6

Manufactured in Canada.

NATIONAL LIBRARY OF CANADA CATALOGUING IN PUBLICATION

Malarek, Victor, 1948–
The Natashas : the new global sex trade / Victor Malarek.

Includes index.
ISBN 0-670-04312-5

1. Prostitution. 2. Child prostitution. 3. Forced labor. I. Title.

HQ117.M34 2003   306.74   C2003-904026-7

Visit the Penguin Group (Canada) website at **www.penguin.ca**

For my daughter, Larissa
With love

Author's Note

These women and girls are victims of rape.
They have suffered enough. To ensure
that they do not endure further humiliation or
embarrassment, their names have been changed.

CONTENTS

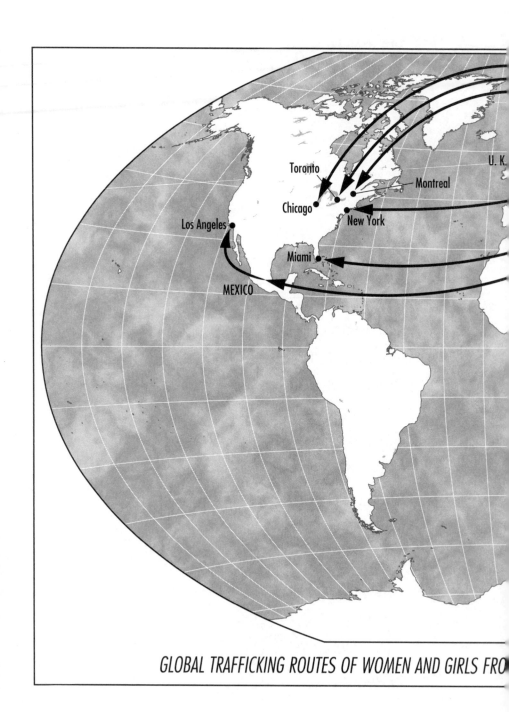

Toronto · Montreal · U. K.

Chicago · New York

Los Angeles · Miami

MEXICO

GLOBAL TRAFFICKING ROUTES OF WOMEN AND GIRLS FRO

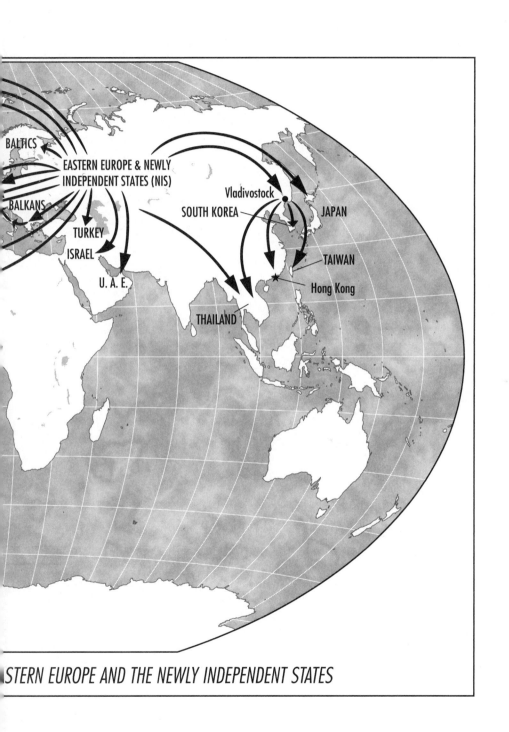

BALTICS

EASTERN EUROPE & NEWLY
INDEPENDENT STATES (NIS)

BALKANS

TURKEY

ISRAEL

U. A. E.

Vladivostock

SOUTH KOREA

JAPAN

TAIWAN

Hong Kong

THAILAND

STERN EUROPE AND THE NEWLY INDEPENDENT STATES

"OH, NATASHA! NATASHA!"

Marika was hit by a blast of hot, dry air as she emerged from the aircraft at Cairo's international airport. The tall, green-eyed, nineteen-year-old blonde looked around, bewildered. Exhausted and nervous, she shuffled into the customs line. An olive-faced officer thumbed through her passport, shot a cursory glance in her direction and stamped an entry visa onto a blank page. When she emerged into the jammed arrival area with her one piece of luggage in hand, she was met by a burly Russian. He grunted her name. She nodded and he grabbed her firmly by the arm, escorting her briskly to a tan, dust-covered, four-wheel-drive jeep.

Crammed in the back seat were three other women—two from Moldova and one from Russia—all in their late teens. The girls were silent. They looked pensive and frightened. The driver shoved Marika into the front passenger side and wedged his beefy gut behind the wheel. "We have no time to waste," he bellowed in Russian. "I have to get to the rendezvous point in two hours."

With a furious lurch, the vehicle lunged forward. The ride was bumpy and deathly quiet. As the jeep barreled deep into the hard-baked, scorching desert, Marika closed her eyes and silently prayed.

Weeks earlier, a garish, rotund woman at a recruitment agency in her hometown of Kharkiv, Ukraine, had spoken excitedly of the job she had arranged for Marika—a stint as a waitress in Tel Aviv. At first, Marika had been apprehensive. She had heard of young women being lured away by jobs that didn't exist only to be forced into prostitution. The recruiter, though, was adamant, swearing up and down—going so far as to invoke the names of Jesus, Joseph and Mary—that this offer was on the up-and-up.

Marika was the perfect dupe. She was desperate for work. Her mother was sick and her father was an unemployed, miserable drunk. Her two younger sisters were wasting away. The job offer was her only chance to make things better. It was a risk; she felt it in every fiber of her body. But it was one she knew she just had to take. The unsettling twist in the job offer was the unusual travel arrangement—a serpentine route that bore the earmarks of an espionage novel. She would be flown from Kyiv to Vienna. There she would switch planes to Cyprus, where she would board another plane for Cairo. Once in Egypt, she was be driven overland to Tel Aviv. Marika voiced her suspicions but the recruiter was persuasive, telling her it had to do with saving huge amounts of money on airfares. Now, after she'd spent two days traveling, Marika's dream of a new job was fading by the mile.

The jeep ground to a stop outside a sun-baked village. The driver leapt out and approached two armed Bedouin men. They exchanged a few words. He handed them an envelope and ordered the women out of the vehicle.

For the first time that day, Marika spoke up. "I said I wanted to go back home," she recalled. "The Russian pig hit me across the face very hard and told me to shut up. My mouth was bleeding and I began to weep."

The driver got back into the jeep and drove off in a cloud of dust, leaving Marika and the other women in the custody of the Bedouin guides. The men were eerie figures, wrapped in tawny robes and scarves with rifles slung over their shoulders and long, curved daggers dangling from their waists. The girls watched in wonder as the men mounted their camels. They barked out an order in Arabic and waved menacingly at the women to follow. The tiny caravan set out across the Sinai Desert, the women scurrying behind the camels on foot.

"It was so hot and we were so very thirsty, but the Arab men taking us across the desert did not care. They kept shouting at us. I have no idea what they were saying. They just yelled," Marika recounted.

They walked for almost two days, stopping twice for meals of pita bread, dried figs and dates and a cup of water, and once to sleep on canvas tarps under the stars.

"I felt what it must have been like for the slaves in the times of the Bible," Marika said. "With every step, I thought I was being punished by God for my past sins."

Late in the second afternoon, the caravan reached an area marked by rusting coils of barbed wire stretching across the barren landscape. The Bedouins dismounted. Jutting up from the sand was a jagged post. They tied their camels to the stump and motioned the women to pick their way over the wire fence. While Marika didn't *know it at the time, they had just reached the Egyptian–Israeli frontier. From there, the tiny band continued on foot. An hour later, the guides suddenly turned to the women and ordered them to drop to the ground. In the distance, Marika could hear the grinding sound of a truck. It was an Israeli army patrol. The Bedouins signaled for them to lie very still. Several tense minutes passed, and the vehicle faded into the distance. Alone once again, the girls scrambled to their feet and, under the watchful eyes of the Bedouins, the trek continued.*

That night, totally spent and dehydrated, the women collapsed under the open sky near the outskirts of a village. One of the guides continued on alone, returning a short while later in a white pickup truck with two Israeli men. The driver spoke fluent Russian and gruffly ordered the women into the back. They were taken to a deserted house and hustled into a bare room. The door was shut and locked behind them. Despite their long, arduous journey, they weren't offered any food or water, nor were they allowed to wash or talk. They slept on the dirt floor.

The next afternoon, two thuggish men showed up and ordered the girls to disrobe. "We were told to take off all our clothes so they could look at us. It was so humiliating," Marika said.

> *We were so frightened. We did as we were told. One of the men took me and the Russian woman. Her name was Lydia. He drove us to Tel Aviv, to an apartment near the sea. Inside were three other women. Two were Ukrainian, the other from Moldova. The door had many locks and a very big man named Avi sat at a desk in the hallway. He was our guard. We were instructed to take a shower, and when we were drying the man came in and told us to put on this cheap lingerie. You could see through it.*

The women were herded into the living room, where their owner addressed them. "We called the owner Talabi. I learned later it means 'owner of the house' in Hebrew. Tal is owner and bi is house," Marika explained.

The brutish man announced that he had purchased them for $10,000 each and that they would be his property until they each paid off a $20,000 debt. He told them they would have to start working off the debt that very evening by servicing clients. He also warned the women that any refusal to do their job would be dealt with swiftly and painfully. To make his point, the owner shot a meaningful glance in Avi's direction. The hairy behemoth guarding the door grinned menacingly at the frightened women.

That night, I felt for the first time what it was to be a whore. I had to service eight men. I felt so terrible and ashamed. I showered after every encounter but I could not wash away the filth in me. Over the next four months, I don't know how many hundreds of Israeli men I was forced to have sex with. Young men, old men, fat, disgusting men. Soldiers, husbands and religious men. It did not matter if I was sick or if I was on my period. I had to work or I would be punished.

During that time Marika tried desperately to find a way to escape, but the windows in the cramped two-bedroom apartment were nailed shut and thick-necked Avi was always on guard.

I pleaded with several clients to help me—the ones who looked sympathetic. I asked to use their cell phone to call my mother, just to tell her I was alive. They all refused, even the religious ones. All they did was complain to Avi if I did not perform to

*their satisfaction. For that, I received a slap in the face, a fine
added to the money I owed for the trip to Israel and nothing to
eat for a day.*

*So often I thought of killing myself, and then I thought of
my poor mother and my sisters. I prayed every day that today I
will be rescued. But the days just passed and passed.*

While servicing the steady stream of clients, Marika found
one thing particularly puzzling. Most didn't distinguish between
the girls' ethnic backgrounds. It didn't matter whether they were
from Russia, Moldova, Romania or Ukraine. In the eyes of the
men, they were all Russian. Even stranger was the way many of
the men addressed them. "They called us Natasha. They never
asked our real name. To them, we were all Natashas.

"We were their sexual fantasy. These fools would walk into the
parlor and with a stupid grin on their face call out 'Natasha!' like
we were some kind of Russian doll. And we were expected to smile
and rush over to them." Marika remembered the first time she was
called by that name.

*This fat, sweaty pig is reaching his climax and he begins to
murmur, "Oh, Natasha! Natasha!" At first I thought it strange
being called by another name. But very soon I came to accept it
as my escape. When I was alone in my thoughts and my dreams,
I was Marika—free from this prison. But when I went with
a man, I became this other woman—this prostitute called
Natasha who was cold and dead inside me.*

*Natasha was my nightmare. Marika was my salvation. I
never told any of these men my real name.*

And they never asked.

INTRODUCTION:
THE FOURTH WAVE

WITH THE BREAKUP of the Soviet Union in 1991 democracy swept
over the republics of this once oppressive Communist empire.
It was a time of immense change and upheaval, yet the majority of the populace seemed up for the challenge. For many, it
was the realization of a lifelong dream. They were free, once
and for all, to live as individual nations. They could speak their
own language, practice their own faiths and, most important,
govern themselves.

Then reality marched in. For much of the population the
dreams of a better way of life evaporated overnight. The move
toward market reforms that was to shepherd these countries
into the fold of the global economy saw a massive flight of
capital instead. Law and order were compromised by corruption, greed and graft. In no time, the economies of the new
republics collapsed and the social safety nets that had provided

a minimum standard of living for the bulk of the population were torn to shreds. Security and equality became relics of the past. Democracy had become a bitter sham.

In the chaos that followed, tens of millions of people were abandoned, left to survive as best as they could. Who could they turn to? Certainly not the government. The ruling class had emerged as the moneyed class. While families worried about their next meal, politicians and top-level bureaucrats lined their pockets until they were bursting at the seams. For them, Mercedes and cell phones became a way of life, their only concerns "how many?" and "which ones?" With those at the nations' helms usurping power and accumulating previously unheard-of wealth, the traditional mistrust of authority, entrenched over decades of Soviet rule, bred widespread disillusionment. The population had to fend for itself.

It didn't take long before the loss of control and the newly porous borders attracted another formidable force. As the once impregnable Iron Curtain disintegrated in shambles, organized crime rushed in . . . and replaced the Curtain with a cheap plastic zipper. The black market skyrocketed and remains endemic today. It also didn't take long for the mob to zero in on the fledgling republics' most valuable assets: beautiful but desperate women and girls—educated, well mannered, with no future in sight.

With the social structure in disarray, families broke down. Children were abandoned in the street. Husbands sought solace in the bottle and alcoholism became an epidemic. Violence against women and children soared. And through it all, the women were left to pick up the pieces. They set out to find work to keep their families together. Even young girls with no families yet of their own went searching for jobs to feed younger siblings and parents. By this time, however, the unemployment rate for women had ballooned to roughly 80 percent. There were simply no jobs to be found. With the stench of desperation in the air, they made perfect targets.

Enter the "saviours," promising endless varieties of what, for these women, was nothing less than salvation. Jobs as nannies in Greece . . . domestics in Italy and France . . . maids in Austria and Spain . . . models in North America and Japan. In each case, the recruiters painted alluring pictures of well-paying jobs in glamorous lands. For this generation of young women, many of whom grew up nursing romantic fantasies of the West, these were more than just dream jobs. They were a way out. Without giving it much thought they jumped at the chance, only to find themselves trapped in a cycle infinitely worse.

The Natashas have been shipped all over the world. They are the latest "It Girls" in the burgeoning business of sex. They line the streets of the red-light districts in Austria, Italy, Belgium and Holland. They stock the brothels in South Korea, Bosnia and Japan. They work nude in massage parlors in Canada and England. They are locked up as sex slaves in apartments in the United Arab Emirates, Germany, Israel and Greece. They star in peep shows and seedy strip clubs in the United States. To the casual observer, they blend in seamlessly with the women who have *chosen* to exchange money for sex. In their cheap makeup, sleazy outfits and stiletto heels, they walk the same walk and talk the same talk. They smile, they wink, they pose and they strut, but they do it because they know what will happen if they don't.

Day in, day out, the Natashas are forced to service anywhere from ten to thirty men a night. The money they make goes to their "owners." They live in appalling conditions, suffering frequent beatings and threats. Those who resist are severely punished. Those who refuse are sometimes maimed or killed.

Most people have no idea that these women even exist. Except for the street trade, they are largely invisible, held behind locked doors in apartments, brothels, massage parlors and bars. To their clients, they are nothing more than an interchangeable body. It doesn't matter that they're enslaved; sex for money is a business transaction. To their owners and pimps, they're perishable goods to be used to the fullest before they spoil. And to the gangs who traffic in these women and girls, they are one of the most profitable forms of business in existence today. Trafficking in human beings is now the third-largest moneymaking venture in the world, after illegal weapons and drugs. In fact, the United Nations estimates that the trade nets organized crime more than $12 billion a year.*

At a roadside coffee bar outside Rome, an Albanian pimp boasted, "I paid $2500 for her. I made my investment back in

---

*All dollar amounts in this book are in U.S. currency.

a few days." According to the international police organization Interpol, a trafficked woman can bring in anywhere from $75,000 to $250,000 a year. From a profit-making perspective, it's the perfect business. Returns are incredible. The goods are plentiful and cheap. And once a woman is spent or no longer in demand, she's discarded and replaced by a younger, fresher face.

The number of victims is staggering. In its 2003 trafficking report, the U.S. State Department points out that "no country is immune from trafficking" and estimates that approximately 800,000 to 900,000 people are trafficked across international borders worldwide. This figure doesn't include internal trafficking, which some observers estimate would raise the number to more than two million. Sadly, the report adds that "human trafficking not only continues but appears to be on the rise worldwide" and that the overwhelming majority of victims are women and children.

It also states that trafficking brutalizes women and children, "exposing them to rape, torture, and to HIV/AIDS and other sexually transmitted and infectious diseases, violence, dangerous working conditions, poor nutrition, and drug and alcohol addiction. Increasing numbers of adults and children trafficked into prostitution as well as street children are contracting HIV/AIDS."

The international bazaar for women is nothing new—Asian women have been the basic commodity for years, and armies of men still flock to Bangkok and Manila on sex junkets. Over the past three decades the world has witnessed four distinct waves of trafficking for sexual exploitation. This latest traffic from Eastern and Central Europe has been dubbed "the Fourth Wave," and the speed and proportion are truly staggering. Just a decade ago, these women didn't even register on the radar screen. Today, they represent more than *25 percent* of the trade.

The first wave of trafficked women came from Southeast Asia in the 1970s and was composed mostly of Thai and Filipino women. The second wave arrived in the early 1980s and was made up of women from Africa, mainly Ghana and Nigeria. The third wave, from Latin America, followed right behind and comprised women mostly from Colombia, Brazil and the Dominican Republic. So it's not that the world has suddenly realized that its women are being kidnapped, sold and raped. The only difference is that today it's flourishing as never before.

The Natashas is an investigation into the latest wave, to find out how it happened and why it continues to thrive. It examines the triggers—the push-pull factors, the supply and the demand—and the wall of complacency, complicity and corruption that has allowed the trade to explode.

In my thirty years as a journalist I've come face to face with scandals, corruption, greed and crime of all kinds. I've seen tragedy of monumental proportions—the desperation of famine, the ravages of war. I've witnessed the loss of life and hope in the Middle East and Africa . . . in Afghanistan, Ethiopia, Somalia and Iran. Yet never before have I been as struck by the senseless disregard for human dignity as I have been these last two years while researching this book.

To me, *The Natashas* is about a generation of lost girls. Virtually every city, town and village in Eastern and Central Europe has seen some of its girls and women disappear. Incredibly, they weren't lost to illness or war or to the tragedy of famine or natural disaster. On the contrary, they have become expendable pawns in the burgeoning business of money, lust and sex. What is most disturbing is that trafficking is a manmade disaster that can be prevented. Yet the world continues to ignore the plight of these women and girls. The time has come to stop the traffic.

1

SMUGGLERS'
PREY

My life is no longer my own.

—LIDA, AN ORPHAN FROM ROMANIA

EVERY DAY, scores of young women throughout the former East Bloc are lured by job offers that lead to a hellish journey of sexual slavery and violence. Despite the barrage of warnings on radio and TV, in newspapers and on billboards, desperate women continue to line up with their naiveté and applications in hand, hoping that, this time, they might just be in luck. Newspaper ads in Kyiv, Bucharest, St. Petersburg, Moscow, Odessa, Minsk and Prague offer destitute women a path out of grinding poverty—a chance at a new start—with no qualifications required. These ads promise a world of relative comfort, especially when compared with conditions at home. Positions

9

are offered around the world as waitresses, models, nannies, dishwashers and maids. The monthly salaries reach $2500, which, for the vast majority, is more than they would ever make in years. Some ads even appear to be officially sanctioned, bearing logos of the American Stars and Stripes or the Canadian Maple Leaf. Others are decked out in the enticing tricolors of Germany, Belgium, the Netherlands, Italy or France.

Bogus recruiters offer prospective job seekers a "complete package" for positions abroad. Typically, they don't require prior work experience, and they almost always seek young, preferably single, women. "Girls: Must be single and very pretty. Young and tall. We invite you for work as models, secretaries, dancers, choreographers, gymnasts. Housing is supplied. Foreign posts available. Must apply in person," an ad in a Kyiv newspaper read. The arrangements often include training, travel documents and airfare, at no cost to the applicants. All they need to do is show up! What these fresh recruits don't know is that in virtually 95 percent of these cases, the jobs being promised do not exist.

Many of the ads are placed by seemingly legitimate employment agencies that have hung out shingles in Russia, Romania, the Czech Republic and Ukraine. Some agencies have gone so far as to set up "career day" booths at universities in Russia, promising profitable work abroad. Most of these firms, or intermediaries, are nothing more than hunting grounds for criminal networks involved in the lucrative industry of sex. For more than a decade, unscrupulous recruiters have snared upward of 175,000 women a year from the former Soviet republics and delivered them as sacrificial lambs to traffickers, pimps and brothel owners in foreign lands.

Women are sometimes recruited in groups, and thinking there is safety in numbers, they enthusiastically sign on. One group of women from Lviv, Ukraine, was offered jobs as housekeepers in the Czech Republic. Once they crossed into the Republic they were sold to a pimp for $500 each and forced into prostitution along the infamous Highway E-55 near the Czech–German border. In another case, an entire dance troupe of young Ukrainian women was conned by an "impresario" promising a five-city European tour. The tour seemed legitimate. They had even been presented with "contracts." They ended up locked in a German apartment and sold into the trade.

In the world of sex trafficking, not all women fall victim to the spin of phony employment agencies and bogus job ads. The first link in the trafficking chain is more often a relative, a neighbor or a friend of a friend. An acquaintance, adept at gaining trust, will approach a young woman's family with an offer to help her land a good job abroad. Every year, tremendous numbers of girls are sucked in by the ruse.

La Strada, a nongovernmental organization in Kyiv that assists trafficked women from Ukraine, has documented numerous cases of deception by acquaintances and individuals in trusted positions in the community. The culprits have included teachers, a local psychologist, the wife of a policeman and the daughter of a village priest.

Tanya, who comes from a small town in the Luhansk region of eastern Ukraine, was one victim of this kind of deception.

Abandoned by her father at the age of four, she set out when she was twenty to find work to help her mother care for an invalid brother. Though she had completed technical school, there was no work to be found since most of the plants and factories in the town had shut down. The situation was desperate. There were times when her family survived on bread and water alone. According to La Strada, Tanya, who was described as "slim and pretty," was offered an incredible opportunity when a friend of her mother's proposed a job abroad in 1998. The woman told Tanya that wealthy Arab families in the United Arab Emirates were hiring maids. These jobs were allegedly paying up to $4000 a month. Tanya couldn't believe her luck.

But when she arrived in Abu Dhabi she was taken to a brothel where a pimp told her that he had bought her for $7000. From that moment on she was to work as a prostitute until she paid off her so-called debt. After three months of captivity, Tanya managed to escape. She bolted to a nearby police station and recounted her tale. Incredibly, she was charged with prostitution and sentenced to three years in a desert prison. In 2001, psychologically crushed and ashamed, Tanya was released. Nothing had happened to her pimp. Branded a prostitute by the Muslim nation, she was summarily deported back to her Ukraine.

In another case documented by La Strada, a twenty-three-year-old university graduate named Olexandra was lured from Chernihiv in northern Ukraine. Olexandra was a divorced mother of a two-year-old daughter and in dire financial straits. She was offered a well-paying job in Germany by a distant relative, who boasted that her own daughter had worked there and had been very happy. And so in the summer of 1997 Olexandra and another young Ukrainian woman crossed into Poland to seek out the work. They were forcibly held in a building where they were beaten and raped. A few weeks later they were smuggled across a river into Germany, where Turkish pimps sold them several times. Along with Polish, Bulgarian and Czech women, Olexandra was forced to service clients in various German brothels. Later that fall the women were arrested in a police raid. Olexandra, now extremely ill, was deported to Ukraine, where she was diagnosed with a severe internal infection, hospitalized for three months and subjected to a number of invasive surgeries. The infection had been caused by her sex servitude abroad. Olexandra's health, tragically, has not returned.

Even more disturbing is the use of trafficked women to lure new victims—the so-called second wave. For many trafficked women, it's the only way of escaping the brutality of being forced to have unwanted sex with a dozen men a day. Their pimps give them the option of returning home if they promise to reel in a number of replacements. And the women are extremely convincing, often pulling up in luxury cars, wearing flashy jewelry and expensive clothes. In no time they're surrounded by envious, naive teenage girls who readily fall for the grandiloquent tales of life in the golden West.

Another trap is the "matchmaking service" operating under the guise of an international introduction firm. These agencies, specializing in "mail-order brides" and often accessible to anyone with a computer, are usually nothing more than online brothels. According to the International Organization for Migration headquartered in Geneva, the vast majority of mail-order-bride agencies in the former Soviet Union are owned and run by organized crime. With countless victims clinging to the fairy-tale hope of a blossoming romance and a better life in the West, the pickings are enormous and ridiculously easy. Women are literally lining up in droves. But when they finally venture out of the country to meet Mr. Right they're delivered into the clutches of ruthless pimps, forced directly into prostitution by their new "husbands" or sold outright for sex.

Other victims have been lured across borders by new "boyfriends," tempted by promises of a night on the town. They too find themselves forced into waiting vehicles, sold to pimps or traffickers for a wad of cash.

Perhaps one of the most terrifying recruitment tactics is outright abduction. The girls are simply taken. In many rural areas in Moldova, Romania and Bulgaria, women and girls have been kidnapped walking home along country roads. The situation is so serious that in some rural areas, parents have stopped sending their daughters to school to protect them from being stolen.

No doubt one of the most appalling aspects of the trade is the targeting of orphans throughout Eastern Europe. In March 2003, for example, the U.S. State Department reported a "pattern of trafficking" involving orphans in Moldova. According to the Country Reports on Human Rights Practices, the girls at risk are those who "must leave orphanages when they graduate," usually at sixteen or seventeen. Most have no source of funds for living expenses or any education or training to get a job. Traffickers often know precisely when these girls are to be turned out of the institutions ("some orphanage directors sold information . . . to traffickers") and are waiting for them, job offers in hand. The State Department also notes that throughout Russia, there are "reports of children being kidnapped or purchased from . . . orphanages for sexual abuse and child pornography" and that child prostitution is "widespread" in orphanages in Ukraine. And in Romania, "many orphanages are complicit in letting girls fall victim to trafficking networks."

Vast armies of Russian children who have run away from brutal orphanages wander the streets of Moscow and St. Petersburg. They are called *Bezprizornye.* Their ranks are swelled by the *Beznadzornye,* street kids who have been abandoned by their parents. These hapless children are the tragic byproducts of the new Russia. According to official estimates there are no fewer than one million; many social workers say the numbers could easily be double that.

The problem, moreover, is permeating all the former Soviet republics. Throughout the Newly Independent States, children are being discarded at an alarming rate by parents and families that can no longer afford to keep them. According to police data in Ukraine, 12,000 children are abandoned by their parents every year. A Ministry of Internal Affairs document states that 100,000 children—14 percent under the age of seven—were registered as homeless in 2000. Half of these children wound up in orphanages. The number of orphans in nearby Romania, meanwhile, exceeds 60,000.

For the most part, these orphanages are nothing more than cold storage facilities. A 1998 Human Rights Watch investigation found that children in Russian orphanages "are exposed to appalling levels of cruelty and neglect. They may be beaten, locked in freezing rooms for days at a time, or sexually abused, and are often subjected to degrading treatment by staff." It's not surprising that thousands of children run away each year, taking their chances by living on the streets.

Orphanages in Ukraine, Romania and Russia are bursting at the seams and, with most having lost their state funding, they're unable to support the crush of orphans they receive. It is a daily struggle to make ends meet. The very principles on which these institutions operate are grossly unsatisfactory and provide little real benefit to a child's chances of leading a normal life after release. It's hard enough attending to the children's basic needs, let alone preparing them for independence once they reach the age of eighteen. Few have training for the drastic changes that life on their own will bring. Most don't even know how to boil a pot of water. This lack of basic life skills makes these children—especially the girls—easy prey for exploiters lurking near the gates. Sometimes they're targeted even before they reach the gate—identified and sold by orphanage workers. Directors of several orphanages in Russia, Ukraine, Romania and the Czech Republic admit their girls are being preyed upon by sex traffickers but lament that they simply don't have the resources to deal with the situation.

In the fall of 1999 two recruiters culled girls from a number of orphanages in the Republic of Karelia in north-western Russia near the Finnish border. The recruiters, looking professional and persuasive, arrived with offers of job training for girls between the ages of fourteen and seventeen. The beleaguered staff was overjoyed that these benevolent souls were taking an interest in the welfare of their girls. They knew full well the harsh reality the girls faced once they were turned out from the institution on their eighteenth birthday, and now at least a handful were being offered a fighting chance of making it on the outside. Following formal interviews, several hopefuls were selected for training in the art of Chinese cooking at a school in China. Their travel and instruction were to be free, with the proviso that they intern for two years as waitresses after their training.

About thirty girls anxiously signed up—all, not surprisingly, pretty, eager and naive. A week later, with their meager possessions, they boarded a bus. The excitement was palpable. And that was it. Instead of heading east to China, the bus barreled south, deep into Western Europe. The destination was a town in Germany, where they were taken to an apartment, locked up and deprived of food and water. The girls' dreams quickly degenerated into a grueling nightmare. They were yelled at constantly. Sometimes they were beaten. A few days later they were herded into the living room and ordered to disrobe before a group of men with bodyguards in tow. The thugs ogled the girls and began bidding, buying the orphans outright in lots of three, four and five. The girls were then distributed to various German brothels, where they were forced to have sex with up to ten men a day. Over a period of six

months, a few managed to escape. Others were scooped up in
police raids. Only then did the story of this horrific deception
make its way back to the orphanages.

It's important to note that in the sordid underbelly of the
international flesh trade, not every woman is an innocent dupe.
In fact, police and government officials often go to great lengths
to stress that some of these women *willingly* enter the trade. In
their eyes, perhaps, this so-called willingness justifies their
apathy and indifference. Nothing, however, could be further
from the truth. Even the "willing" women have no idea of what
really awaits. It's true that many women know full well when
they accept a job offer that they'll be working in some aspect of
the sex industry—massage parlors, strip clubs, peep shows and
escort agencies. Depending on who's assessing the situation—
police, social workers, bureaucrats or women's rights groups—
the estimates of how many sign on "knowingly" range from 30
to 80 percent. Yet the vast majority of these women aren't aware
of the exact nature or conditions of the work. Those who agree
to work abroad as prostitutes and escorts are led to believe they
will do so under specific conditions. They're told they will earn
$5000 a month, live in a luxury apartment, have two days off a
week, service two or three clients a night and never have to go
with a man they don't like. The "contract" is often for a mere
three months, at which point the women are told that they will
be free to leave.

Many of these women venture out with visions of the film
Pretty Woman dancing in their heads. They expect to rake in lots
of fast money and in the process perhaps even meet Mr. Right.

But those fantasies are shattered when, within moments of arriving at their destinations, they learn their true fate. Most end up in situations of incredible debt bondage, unable to earn enough to pay back the high interest on their travel and living expenses. They become victims of the worst possible forms of sexual exploitation. They are *not* free to leave, nor can they easily escape. They are sold to pimps or brothel owners on the open market, and soon find themselves trapped in abusive situations in which they are forced to have sex with as many as ten, twenty or thirty clients a day. They cannot refuse a customer or a demand. They are not allowed sick days. They do not get time off for their period. Some end up pregnant and having abortions. Many acquire HIV or other sexually transmitted diseases, not to mention the psychological and medical problems that come from constant abuse and gang rape. Some become alcoholics. Others become drug addicts. Often their pimps addict them to heroin to ensure they comply with all their demands.

All in all, no matter how "willing" they were and regardless of how they fell into the trafficking trap, the vast majority of these women end up as nothing more than slaves—abused, used and traded. And when they're no longer useful or when they've gotten too old or too sick and riddled with disease, they are simply discarded. Only then can they contemplate returning home. Countless others never do go home. Many die from the abuse and the diseases. Others give up and kill themselves.

ONCE THESE WOMEN ARE RECRUITED—or captured or stolen—a well-oiled trafficking system kicks into gear. Criminal organizations use a variety of mechanisms to transport their human cargo across international borders. Many do so via channels that seem completely legal, thanks to student, tourist or temporary work visas. In some countries, women can get visas to work as exotic dancers or artists. Others enter as "mail-order brides." They then overstay their visas and slip into the netherworld of illegal migrants.

When these seemingly legal avenues aren't available, however, the traffickers turn to professional smugglers. Organized crime groups have established a massive and intricate network of routes through which they move women to different countries by land, water and air. These smuggling routes literally crisscross the globe and are controlled virtually every step of the way by interconnected criminal networks. In fact, most of the routes were carved out long ago by traffickers to smuggle illegal weapons or drugs. The recent explosive demand for Eastern and Central European women has simply attracted another black-market commodity to these well-trodden paths.

Professional traffickers, used to circumventing border crossings, engage border authorities in a never-ending game of cat and mouse. They constantly vary their routes to keep one step ahead of the law, moving the women across borders with relative ease. Along the serpentine border of the European Union, smugglers have established a complex system of well-protected corridors by exploiting "green borders" or unguarded frontiers. One of the more significant overland corridors is known as "the Eastern Route" and winds through Poland and into Germany. Once the traffickers and their victims are inside the European Union, all member nations are fair game and movement for organized crime becomes relatively unfettered. The women smuggled through this route come from Russia, Ukraine, Romania, Latvia, Lithuania and Estonia, and are found in disturbing numbers in Italy, Greece, Germany, Belgium, Austria and France.

The most notorious corridor is the Balkan route. It weaves its way through Serbia, Croatia, Albania, Macedonia, Bosnia-Herzegovina, Montenegro and Kosovo. During the bloody civil war that ripped the former Yugoslavia apart, criminal organizations established a strong foothold in the region. Their illicit contraband involved weapons and drugs. With the fighting now over, the Balkan route is used to smuggle illegal drugs, cars and women. This clandestine route traverses the Balkan territory, the key destination being the European Union. Italy is a prime target, providing easy access to many of the other countries in Europe. The Balkans, however, aren't just transit points, thanks to the massive influx of United Nations peacekeepers and international humanitarian aid workers. Shockingly, their presence has provided a valuable, readymade market for local brothel keepers trading in trafficked women.

In Moldova, the path to sexual servitude often starts in a tiny, impoverished village, moving swiftly through Romania and into Hungary or Montenegro. Then it's on to processing centers in Serbia. Women from Ukraine, on the other hand, are usually taken to Belgrade through Hungary and then distributed to Bosnia or Italy. Romanians cross into Serbia at the Iron Gates on the Danube River, while Bulgarian women are usually smuggled directly into the country. The route from Serbia to Italy is either overland—through Bosnia, Croatia and Slovenia—or through the Albanian seaport towns of Vlorë and Durres, where women cling to high-speed rubber dinghies charging across the Adriatic Ocean to the Italian coast.

Another key corridor leads from the southern Bulgarian "golden triangle" of Blagoevgrad, Sandanski and Petric to Greece. Young women from Russia, Romania, Georgia and Ukraine are moved by trafficking rings into a number of hotels in these Bulgarian towns. They're met by Greek gangsters who arrive in a regular stream to choose and place their orders, and even to test them out first-hand. The women are then entrusted to local smugglers, adept at navigating the treacherous mountain routes on the Greek–Bulgarian border, and are delivered to their new owners. Other trafficked women are destined for Turkey, yet another bustling market for Eastern European women, especially Ukrainians. To get to Turkey, traffickers travel overland through Georgia and Bulgaria and on boats from the Ukrainian Black Sea port of Odessa en route to Istanbul and Ankara. Traffickers have also carved out smuggling routes through the Baltic States into the Scandinavian countries.

The geography and circumstance of trafficking women, however, is fluid and ever changing. At the beginning of the 1990s the prime sending countries were Hungary, the Czech Republic and Poland. A decade later these remain important countries of origin but have also become major destination points. Most of the women trafficked into the Czech Republic and Poland come from Russia, Ukraine, Belarus, Moldova,

Romania, Georgia and Bulgaria. Meanwhile, the former Soviet Republics of Central Asia—Armenia, Georgia, Azerbaijan, Kyrgyzstan and Kazakhstan—are now emerging recruitment zones. One-third of the traffic from these regions moves through Central Europe and then onward to other European countries, while the remainder heads to the Middle East and China. In these directions, too, there is no shortage of routes.

Organized crime syndicates have also plotted lucrative and complex routes to far-flung destinations to capitalize on their "goods." Israel, the United Arab Emirates, South Korea, Thailand, China and Japan are all key to their prostitution rackets. Canada and the United States are becoming increasingly significant destinations for trafficked women from Eastern Europe, as evidenced by the scores of ads in the back pages of cheesy tabloids in numerous North American cities. "Full-service nude massages by Russian beauties" are offered at $60 an hour—touching is permitted and customers are guaranteed "a release." The ads also show a huge increase in Russian escort services in New York, Miami, Chicago, Los Angeles, Montreal and Toronto, and in each of these cities, Russian dancers have become a popular staple in strip clubs and peep shows. The procurers make no distinction between Russian, Ukrainian, Latvian or Lithuanian women. They simply lump them together into one ethnic mold—Russian.

In order to keep one step ahead of the law and the pressure from international authorities to tighten border entry points, organized crime is moving increasingly into internal markets. Many women are being trafficked into the very cities from

which the traffickers recruit. Major East European cities such as
Bucharest, Prague, Odessa, Kyiv, St. Petersburg and Moscow
are offering the burgeoning sex tourism market from North
America, Europe and Asia a steady supply of East European
women. Women are also being transported to Czech, Polish
and Hungarian towns and roadways near the border with
Germany and Austria to cash in on the regular cross-border
traffic. The most notorious roadway is Highway E-55.

Renowned worldwide, Highway E-55 lies alongside the
main thoroughfare between Dresden and Prague just a few kilometers from the Czech–German border. To motorists, this
miserable five-kilometer stretch of asphalt boasts one of the
highest concentrations of prostitutes in Europe. For those
driven by lust, it has been dubbed the "highway of love," its
main customers German and Austrian men driving in for the
great "deals." They come for the cut-rate prices—half of what
they pay in their homelands. A half-hour off E-55 or in nearby
Dubi costs about $35. For sex without a condom, it's an extra
$10. But it's not just the Europeans who come here. With the
highway's notoriety plastered on countless websites, sex tourists
from as far away as Australia and North America are jetting to
Germany, renting cars and cruising in. Every parking spot and
meter of roadside is divvied up and controlled by pimps; every
shaded lair in the nearby woods serves as an open-air brothel—
day and night.

I decided to drive in for a first-hand look and was immediately struck by the sheer numbers of merchants lined up on
both sides of the roadway hawking their wares. The scene was

surreal. The merchants were unusually young. Some were quite striking. All were women and girls from Ukraine, Romania, Russia, Belarus and Bulgaria. Their wares were their bodies, in various degrees of undress. They posed salaciously in skin-tight, midriff-baring jeans, skimpy halters and stiletto heels. As the steady stream of motorists whizzed by, women pulled up their T-shirts and flashed their breasts. Others shouted at the passersby, promising to do whatever they ask.

Despite the macabre, circus-like atmosphere, what is evident even to the untrained observer is that the majority of these women are not in control of their trade. Prowling the territory in beat-up cars are men in sweat suits with gold chains dangling around their necks. Their only function is to keep a watchful eye on their merchandise and collect the money they make.

As I stared in stunned silence at the hapless sea of humanity on E-55, several women gingerly stepped into the street and yelled at passing drivers, *"Warte mal!"* (Hey, wait!) and *"Ich mache alles!"* (I do everything!). A slim, blond woman with shoulder-length hair darted over to my car. As I slowed down in the crush of traffic, she pulled open the door and jumped into the passenger side. With a wave of her hand, she directed me to drive over to a secluded, wooded area where she demanded 1400 Czech crowns in advance. I did as she said but told her that I just wanted to talk. She looked dumbfounded, but shrugged her shoulders and nodded.

Throughout the brief, fifteen-minute encounter, her hard brown eyes never left the dashboard. Picking nervously at her raw cuticles, she spoke in a whisper. The conversation was labored. Her name was Lida. She was Romanian, eighteen years old and had been working E-55 for three months. She was an orphan. As she had been preparing to leave an orphanage just outside Bucharest, a woman showed up claiming to be a relative.

"She was my aunt. The director said it was so. I didn't believe her but what could I do? She told me she had permission to take me. I went with her. She took me to Stephan and he put me to work on this road. I had no say in the matter. My life is no longer my own," she said in a resigned tone.

Suddenly her eyes filled with panic. "If he sees me talking to you, he will beat me."

I asked if she wanted to escape. "I can take you away from here."

Lida's hands began to shake. "No. He will find me and then he will kill me. He has sworn that to me. Please, I don't want to talk anymore."

The conversation ended abruptly when she suddenly dove under the dashboard, making it appear she was working. From the corner of her eye she'd caught a glimpse of Stephan in the passenger-side mirror. The beady-eyed pimp with oily, kinky black hair and a repugnant sneer cruised by in a white, beat-up Ford Opel. He stared menacingly in my direction. A few minutes later Lida left the car and scurried back to her spot on E-55. She looked troubled and sad. Her pimp pulled up, rolled down his window and began yelling at her. Then he stuck his hand out the window and flicked his fingers. She passed him the 1400 crowns and he sped off. With a smile pasted back on her face, Lida stepped into the road, waved at the next passing German license plate and shouted, *"Ich mache alles!"*

My next stop was the nearby Bohemian hamlet of Dubi. Once famous for its blue-and-white, onion-shaped porcelain known as "cibulak," it is now infamous for loose women. Dubi is anything but charming. Bars with names like Alibi, Libido and Kiss line the main street alongside a string of fleabag hotels and pensions where no one stays the night. Since the opening of Germany's borders in 1989 the number of prostitutes working on the Czech side of the border has mushroomed. There are a score of bars and each has a dozen or more young women sitting at tables or dancing to disco music as they wait for the next man to arrive. Over a glass of cheap wine negotiations are quickly finalized, followed by giggles and a little groping before the twosome head off to a room above or at the back of the bar.

"This region is a sex zoo," a police officer said acidly. "Nobody in government is interested in stopping it. So why should I bother? My job is to make certain there is no trouble, and these whores know better than to make trouble."

I asked if he thought many of the women were trafficked and forced to work as prostitutes.

The officer laughed. "They have a choice to be prostitutes or to live the good life. They have chosen to be whores."

A little farther down the roadway in the picturesque hills of the Bohemian Highlands is the spa resort town of Teplice. It harbors a dark secret—the tragic consequences of the sordid romps on E-55 and in Dubi. Every year, dozens of unwanted babies are born and abandoned at the local hospital. They're the result of clients willing to pay a little more for sex without a condom, and of women who aren't given any money from their pimps to purchase alternative birth control. On average, three prostitutes give birth each month. Many of the babies are born with syphilis or are HIV-positive. Some are drug addicted. A doctor at the hospital noted that abortions are costly and that many of the women work right up to the day they go into labor. In fact, a steady stream of clients comes specifically to have sex with pregnant women, and they're willing to pay a premium for the opportunity.

Nearby in a beleaguered orphanage, about seventy E-55 babies are on display, awaiting adoption.

2

THE
BREAKING GROUNDS

*I knew I did not have the strength to endure
what would surely follow if I resisted.*
—SOPHIA, WHO WAS "TRAINED" AFTER
HER THIRD DAY IN CAPTIVITY

OLEKSANDER MAZUR KNOWS all about the breaking grounds. A Ukrainian police officer, he was assigned to the United Nations international police force—CIVPOL—in Pristina, the capital of Kosovo. His job was to kick down the doors of brothels and rescue trafficked women in this renegade Serbian province. For a little more than a year he did just that, and in that time he rescued more than a hundred women—most of them mere teenagers.

"I would like to clean up this mess for good," Mazur said. "I would like not to have this job. It has cost me my dreams."

From numerous investigations, Mazur has compiled an impressive dossier on the traffickers and their operations. He knows the enemy well—what it looks like, how it thinks, how it moves. He knows the names of several key players; their descriptions are etched in his mind. More important, he's figured out the locations of secret training centers in Serbia where these thugs snap the spirit and will of their terrified hostages. These centers lie within his grasp, but he is absolutely powerless. His mandate is limited to Kosovo. The breaking grounds, just a few kilometers across the border in Serbia, are in neither his job description nor his jurisdiction.

> I would love to have the power, the authority to go into Serbia and catch the criminals and shut them down for good. Here it's like getting the street-level drug dealer. It's frustrating, especially when you know you can get the main traffickers but you are not allowed to cross the border. I've got a lot of information. It is not such a big deal to catch them. You just go there and break down the gate.
>
> Belgrade is the main center in Serbia. There are also apartments in Nis and Kraljevo. There are places there that are like prisons, where hundreds of young women are held until they're sold. It is there the girls are broken. It is where they are trained. Those places are hell.

Anna Eva Radicetti has also heard about the Serbian breaking grounds through her interviews with scores of rescued women. As manager of the Counter-Trafficking Return and Reintegration project of the International Organization for

Migration in Kosovo, she too has gathered reams of information about what happens to trafficked women on the other side of the border. "There are big apartments or houses in Belgrade where most girls are brought. Sometimes there are fifty girls in each place," she explained. Radicetti has learned that potential buyers "test-drive" the women, much like the way we test-drive new cars. "They are sex-tested by each buyer. They want to see for themselves what the girls can do in terms of sex performance."

When they're not being used, she said, the young hostages are poked and prodded like cattle.

> They have to stand naked for hours a day while men come and look them over. They look at their breasts, the color of their skin and check to see if they have rashes or pimples. The girls have to dress up to look like prostitutes and put on makeup. Those who resist are isolated, beaten and terrorized. It's even more humiliating for them if they are considered ugly. They are treated worse than animals with what they are forced to do. You have a full range of traffickers, from cruel to vicious.

What happens to most trafficked women, whether they were tricked, abducted or willing, is criminal. They are forced into situations of profound terror, comparable to being held hostage. They are immediately deprived of their travel documents and their every movement is tightly controlled and restricted. Usually they live on the premises, where they work, locked in rooms, under constant guard and in fear of extreme violence and threats. They are warned that if they try to escape, they will be found and severely punished. They are also told that their families will be targeted. Often they're videotaped or photographed in embarrassing sexual encounters, and warned that if they escape, the pictures will be sent to their families and distributed around their hometowns.

SOPHIA RECOILED WITH SHEER PANIC when asked about her abduction at knifepoint while walking home one evening on a rural road about a kilometer from her home.

"I could hear the car approaching and suddenly I froze. I could not move," the eighteen-year-old Romanian said, nervously spinning her shoulder-length black hair in her fingers as she recounted the nightmare that became her life for the next four months.

> Two men with knives forced me into the car. I thought they would rape me and then kill me. I prayed that my life would be spared. Instead, I was driven to a river crossing where they sold me to a Serbian man. He took me across the Danube River in a small boat and then to an apartment in a town in the mountains. I don't know the name. But I soon learned I was in Serbia.

Sophia was horrified by what she witnessed during her brief imprisonment in the building. Her experiences continue to haunt her in her sleep, and are typical of what women encounter in the breaking grounds.

There were so many young girls in there. They were from
Moldova, Romania, Ukraine and Bulgaria. Some were
crying. Others looked terrified. We were told not to speak to
each other. Not to tell each other our names or where we
were from. All the time, very mean and ugly men came in
and dragged girls into rooms. Sometimes they would rape
girls in front of us. They yelled at them, ordering them to
move certain ways . . . to pretend excitement . . . to moan . . .
It was sickening.

Every single girl was physically and emotionally abused by
the heartless goons who ran the center.

Those who resisted were beaten. If they did not cooperate,
they were locked in dark cellars with rats with no food or
water for three days. One girl refused to submit to anal sex,
and that night the owner brought in five men. They held her
on the floor and every one of them had anal sex on her in
front of all of us. She screamed and screamed, and we all
cried.

The next day, the girl tried to hang herself.
"Many girls attempted suicide," Sophia said. "I was told a
few were successful and their bodies were buried in the woods."
Sophia's biggest fear was being broken in herself.

I dreaded that moment. In the first day, I thought to myself,
I will fight back. Then I saw what they did to one girl who
refused. She was from Ukraine. Very beautiful, very strong-
willed. Two of the owners tried to force her to do things

and she refused. They beat her, burned her with cigarettes all over her arms. Still she refused. The owners kept forcing themselves on her and she kept fighting back. They hit her with their fists. They kicked her over and over. Then she went unconscious.

She just lay there, and they still attacked her anally. When they finished, she didn't move. She wasn't breathing. There was no worry on the faces of the owners. They simply carried her out.

A couple of days after the Ukrainian girl had been taken away, one of her compatriots dug deep for the courage to ask about her. The owner's reaction was sharp, swift and brutal.

He grabbed her by the hair and dragged her outside. When she returned, she looked like she had stared death in the face. She told us the owner took her to a forest not far from the building, handed her a shovel and instructed her to dig. She believed she was digging her own grave. As she dug, she noticed a fresh mound of earth beside her. She was certain this was the grave of the Ukrainian girl.

After an hour, the man snatched the shovel from the girl's hands and ordered her out of the shallow pit. His message was clear: "Ask any more questions and you will end up in the grave."

On her third day of captivity, Sophia was "trained." She submitted without resistance. She moved as she was told. She feigned excitement at every thrust.

I knew I did not have the strength to endure what would surely follow if I resisted. That night, I just wanted to die. I was so humiliated. To these men, I was just a piece of meat. From that moment on, I have felt like filth. I cannot wash that feeling from my body or my mind no matter how hard I try.

A week later, Sophia was sold to a pimp along with two other women. She was now his. She knew him only as Saba, a twenty-something Albanian. The three were taken by truck into Albania and then smuggled into Italy in the dead of night on a speedboat across the Adriatic. Saba was a particularly nasty sort, with a penchant for threatening his "property" with burning cigarettes. He put the women to work on Via Salaria, a busy roadway leading into the Eternal City. They were housed in a damp basement apartment where they slept on foam mattresses. The pimp kept all the earnings, except for a small stipend for basic necessities and food. "For certain, he made a thousand dollars a night from us," Sophia said. "We were not permitted to return to the apartment until he had that much money."

Three months later, with the help of a sympathetic regular, Sophia ran away and was taken to a Catholic rescue mission in southern Italy.

FOR HUNDREDS OF "BROKEN IN" WOMEN trafficked from Eastern Europe, the next stop on the road is the infamous Arizona Market. Between Sarajevo and Zagreb, in northwest Bosnia near the frontier with Serbia and Croatia, there lies a stretch of road called Arizona Highway. Beside it is Arizona Market. With its narrow alleyways and hundreds of pine-fronted stalls, it resembles an American gold-rush town from the 1800s. During the day it bustles with throngs of eager shoppers navigating a labyrinth of dirt roads in search of a bargain. Here you can find not only T-shirts, shoes, makeup, mattresses, ghetto blasters and pirated CDs, but also knock-off brand names like Rolex, Levi's and Ralph Lauren, dried fruit, gleaming porcelain toilet bowls and freshly killed chickens.

At the entrance a large sign pays homage to the Americans: "Our thanks to the U.S. Army for supporting the development of this market." Constructed in 1996 after the Balkan civil war, the market—often jokingly referred to as the Wal-Mart of Bosnia—was the brainchild of an American general. It was envisioned as a place where all factions—Croats, Serbs and Bosnians—could set aside their ethnic and religious rivalries and come together in the spirit of free trade. In the daytime, with its hordes of shoppers, the market looks like an experiment that has somehow gone right. But when the sun goes down a more pernicious trade kicks into gear.

In the shadows of night, the T-shirts and shoes are replaced by luxury cars and SUVs stolen off the streets of the European Union, not to mention weapons, illegal drugs and black-market cigarettes by the truckload. But the most valuable goods are the ones with a pulse—young women and girls trafficked from Eastern Europe.

Mara Radovanovic, vice-president of Lara, a local women's group in nearby Bijeljina, shakes her head in disgust at the

Arizona Market. "That is when the traders come to buy girls. They order the girls to take off all their clothes and they are standing in the road naked. They are exposed to be purchased like cattle." Radovanovic said trafficked women are also sold at "sex slave auctions" in nightclubs with names like Acapulco and Las Vegas that have sprung up inside the market. "The girls appear naked on stage with numbers in their hands. Men walk up, touch their flesh, inspect their skin and even look into their mouths before they make a bid." Once purchased, the women are held in slavery-like conditions and forced to work in bars and brothels throughout the region. "Their personal documents are taken away and they are not permitted to go out without a guard. They are paid no money at all, and often nightclub owners force them to have sex with clients without protection. As a consequence, every week there is at least one of those women undergoing an abortion in the Bijeljina hospital."

In the surrounding hamlets, "collection centers" have emerged where hundreds of women are held captive in the basements, cellars and attics, awaiting their turn on the auction block. "Most of them are young, naive girls from rural areas who believe that they will find a job across the border," Radovanovic said. "They realize what kind of job they have to do only when they end up in the Arizona Market or in Serbia. By then it is too late and they have little chance to escape."

The women are sold to the hundreds of brothels and bars that pepper the countryside throughout Bosnia-Herzegovina. There they service the locals and, more significantly, the huge numbers of foreigners who make up the international peacekeeping and reconstruction forces. Those women who aren't purchased on the auction block end up staying in Arizona, catering to shoppers and local policemen at a dozen clubs in the market.

At an urgent one-day meeting in late fall 2001 sponsored by Radovanovic's group, the local police were invited to speak about law enforcement efforts to end the trade. Within minutes, the two male officers were put on the hot seat. Surrounded on all sides by determined women—all volunteers with local and regional NGOs—they were asked, point-blank, why the police simply sit back when it's obvious what's occurring in virtually every town in the area. Looking uncomfortable, the officers summoned one pathetic excuse after another, citing conflicting laws and regulations covering the various jurisdictions. But Radovanovic grilled the men relentlessly. She accused the police, straight out, of complicity and corruption, pointing out that a strip bar reputed to harbor trafficked girls operated with impunity directly across from the Bijeljina police station. The officers squirmed but stuck to their script.

Later that evening, a law student took me to that very bar. It was dimly lit, smoke filled and reeked of body odor and cheap beer. Disco music crackled from two speakers perched on an elevated stage where a naked teenage girl moved awkwardly to the thumping beat. As she danced, she stared at herself in a floor-to-ceiling mirror at the edge of the stage. She looked morose and self-conscious. It was as though she was in a trance, and that the young woman she saw in the reflection was a stranger who had stolen her body.

A meaty bouncer escorted us to a booth at one end of the bar. From the corner of my eye I noticed the owner—a slug with a buzz cut in a black leather jacket—wave his hand at two girls sitting at a table near the front. They jumped up and rushed over to our table. "What is it you want?" a pale-looking girl with short brown hair asked in Ukrainian.

"Two beers," I replied, realizing a second after responding in Ukrainian that it was clearly the wrong thing to say. The girl stared at me, wide-eyed, and retreated to the bar, exchanging furtive words with the owner. He picked up his cell phone and punched in a number. "I think we should drink our beers quickly and get out of here," I told my companion. He nodded anxiously.

At that moment, another young woman took to the stage. She was obese and clearly on display for the sport and ridicule of the patrons. Holding on to a brass pole, she bounced to the music while a phalanx of men at the edge of the stage whistled and laughed. While she spun her way around the pole, the previous dancer reappeared from a back room in a beige negligee. The owner ordered her to a darkened corner where a greasy middle-aged man sat hunched over a bottle of cheap red wine. The moment she sat down he started groping her, forcing his hand up and down her top. As he pawed her she kept her eyes closed, as if in prayer. A moment later, the two retreated to a room behind the bar.

We were just finishing our drinks when five local goons sauntered over to our table. One of them said something to me. The tone was definitely threatening. I turned to my guide.

"He wants to know who you are and why we are here."

"Tell him we were thirsty and came in for a beer."

A number of words were exchanged. "He said to finish the beer and get out of here. He doesn't like your face."

We got up and left.

THE LEVEL OF PHYSICAL VIOLENCE and psychological intimidation used to control these women is deliberate and extreme. It's meant to instill fear—to crush them, destroy their will, force them to comply. There are reports of women being mutilated and murdered as punishment for refusing to engage in the sex trade. Women have been killed as examples to other women for daring to resist. According to Italian police, a foreign prostitute is murdered each month in that country alone. In Istanbul, Turkey, two Ukrainian women were thrown off a high-rise balcony while six Russian captives watched in horror. In Serbia, a Ukrainian woman was purportedly beheaded in front of a group of trafficked girls. A Russian woman was strangled by her pimp in May 1996 when she refused to hand over a $20 tip she received from a client. Her Israeli pimp dumped her body near the West Bank town of Ramallah so that police would believe she had been murdered by Arabs. And in 2000, the bodies of two Moldovan women were found floating in a river near the Arizona Market. Their hands were tied behind their backs, their feet attached to concrete blocks and their mouths taped shut—all marks of execution-style killings. On the tape over their mouths, their killers had scrawled the words "Organization for Security and Co-operation in

Europe." Under its mandate, the OSCE has been trying to bring civil order to Bosnia-Herzegovina.

Then there are the countless cases of women like Irini Penkina, who simply give up and take their own lives. The appalling circumstances behind Irini's suicide in Greece rocked the cradle of democracy, but the public outrage was short-lived. The twenty-year-old from Belarus was found dead in an apartment in the northern port city of Thessalonica in October 1998. A perfunctory police investigation concluded that she had killed herself in despair at being forced by her Greek pimp to service more than a dozen men a day. Irini knotted black pantyhose around her neck and strung the other end around a pipe above the toilet bowl in her closet-sized bathroom. Her twenty-three-year-old roommate found her body. There was no suicide note.

Investigators learned that she had left her homeland with the promise of a waitressing job in Greece. When she arrived, she was brutalized into submission and then imprisoned in a stifling bordello in a town notorious for prostitution. She and three other women—a Bulgarian, a Moldovan and a Ukrainian—were rarely allowed to leave the apartment, except under the watchful eye of a thuggish guard. Their pimp forced them to service a blur of sex tourists and locals scurrying into the dank apartment at all hours of the day and night. He was arrested and charged with luring the women into prostitution and procuring them, but was later acquitted for lack of evidence.

IN EVERY METROPOLIS around the globe, trafficked girls mingle freely with the women who *choose* to take money for sex. On the surface, it's hard to tell them apart. They dress and look the same. They have the same inviting expression. They smile, they pose, they flaunt and they strut. That's what prospective clients and the public see in the bars or streets.

But that's also what the pimps *make certain* they see. What they miss entirely is the darker side of the trade. It's an ugly side, hidden behind heavy padlocked doors in rooms with iron bars on the windows and armed thugs in the hall. There, the striking blonde smiling coyly on the street may have been beaten with electrical wires the evening before. Behind these walls, the sweet-looking brunette who stands shyly on a corner with the innocent gaze of seventeen-year-old schoolgirl may have just been indoctrinated into the trade by two guards and a pimp intent on "breaking her in." *This* is the side that keeps them on the street and *this* is the side that keeps the smiles on their lips. They stay because they fear what will happen if they run . . . and they smile because they know what will happen if they don't.

If their "clients" looked closely at the bodies they're using, they just might see some of the telltale signs—bruises peeking through under cheap flesh-colored makeup, whip marks on the buttocks, cigarette burns on the arms. If they paused long enough, while reaching their climax, to actually look into these women's eyes, they might see frustration, revulsion, fear, depression, resignation, anger, shame . . . And if they asked the woman they're with why she does what she does and actually took the time to dig into her past, they might hear how she was kidnapped from an orphanage in Ukraine, smuggled out of the country, sold at an auction and forced onto the street by a money-grubbing pimp who forces her to bring in $500 a night.

In short, they're forced to do whatever it takes with whoever asks, as long as he pays, and they're forced to do it with a smile on their face, a sparkle in their eyes and a moan on their lips . . . exactly as trained in the breaking grounds.

3

CRIMINAL
INTENT

You can buy a woman for $10,000 and you can make
your money back in a week if she is pretty and
she is young. Then everything else is profit.
—A NOTORIOUS MOBSTER KNOWN AS TARZAN

IN THE SOURCE COUNTRIES of Russia, Ukraine, Moldova and
Eastern Europe, the illegal trafficking of women is fueled by
a desperate need for a better life. In the destination nations,
it is driven by an insatiable, self-indulgent appetite for
purchased sex. The force that brings them together is organized crime, notorious for reacting swiftly to attractive market
forces. But in this situation, unlike the illegal trade of guns
and drugs, the risks for criminals are minimal and the profits
extremely high.

Anna Diamantopoulou, European commissioner responsible for Employment and Social Affairs, lamented the savagery
of modern-day trafficking in a speech to an anti-trafficking
conference in Brussels in September 2002:

> It is a booming industry, run with ruthless efficiency by
> powerful, multinational criminal networks . . . These are not
> casual criminals. They run well-funded, well-organized,
> influential organizations. They know their business inside
> out and respond to changes in the market with a speed
> unmatched by even the most competitive corporations.
> Their expertise and their ability to exploit the market are
> surpassed only by their disregard for human life. Women
> are bought, sold and hired out like any other product. The
> bottom line is profit.

The profits are, in fact, unseemly. Interpol estimates that
each exploited woman can bring in $75,000 to $250,000 a
year. Pimps often brag that a woman purchased for $1500 can
bring in $100 an hour . . . making back their investment in just
a few nights. According to Willy W. Bruggeman, deputy director of the European Union–wide police intelligence agency
Europol, the trade in human beings earns up to $12 billion
euros worldwide every year.

The trade is also widespread. Bruggeman notes that all
member states of the European Union "have reported the presence of foreign OC [organized crime] groups" in the trafficking
of human beings. And it's not just Europe. As head of the UN
Office for Drug Control and Crime Prevention in 2001, Pino

Arlacchi observed that trafficking in human beings is "one of the most globalized markets in the world today . . . one that almost no country is immune from." Arlacchi also pointed out that as the fastest-growing international crime, "it is now the third most profitable business for organized crime, behind drugs and arms."

The outlook is sobering. Organized crime groups are increasingly moving toward large hierarchical structures. They no longer want to deal with middlemen. They want to run the schemes for themselves—from recruitment to final exploitation. According to Europol's 2002 Crime Assessment report dealing with Trafficking in Human Beings into the European Union, this will "increase the profitability, efficiency and security of operations." It also "reflects a desire to be more in control of all elements of the trade, perhaps indicating the elevation of trafficking in human beings within the wider portfolio of OC criminal activity."

Urgent cables, reports and alerts from criminal intelligence–gathering agencies and police forces around the world paint a frightening picture of these heightened activities. The most formidable threat to vulnerable Slavic women today is Russian Organized Crime (ROC). Wherever women and girls from Eastern European countries are being trafficked, the iron fist of ROC is sure to be playing a hand. Their syndicates, now numbering more than 200, are active in fifty-eight countries around the world, including Austria, Germany, Belgium, Holland, Italy, Hungary, Poland, Turkey, Israel, Canada and the United States. Most have their grip on prostitution rackets, though they're also behind huge extortion and fraud schemes.

These ROC syndicates have formed a powerful global criminal axis with the four principal powers in international organized crime: the Italian Mafia, the Colombian drug cartels, the Chinese Triads and the Japanese Yakuza. According to Italian police, in some parts of Italy ROC's influence is already greater than that of the Mafia. The Russian mobs have also established strategic alliances with U.S. crime groups and biker gangs and with Ukrainian, Polish, Hungarian, Czech, Turkish, Serbian, Israeli and Albanian gangs.

Political leaders in that corner of the world are repeatedly citing ROC's increasing involvement in the trafficking of women from Eastern Europe. Bulgarian Interior Ministry Chief Secretary Bozhidar Popov stated publicly that Russian criminals are using his country as a transit point to move Russian, Ukrainian, Georgian and Chechen women into Turkey, Greece and Western Europe for prostitution. Lithuanian Member of Parliament Vilija Aleknaite-Abramikiene reported that Russian goons are behind the trafficking of women for the sex industry in his country. One of the more notorious gangs under intense investigation by several European police forces is the powerful Izmailovskaya syndicate. Another group, the feared Mogilevich organization, runs strip clubs in Prague, Riga and Kyiv; the clubs are teeming with trafficked women. In Russia's Far East, vicious gangs in Vladivostok direct the supply of women to brothels and clubs in Hong Kong, Taiwan, South Korea, Thailand and Macao. Roughly a dozen Russian-run prostitution rings are currently operating in Israel. A November 1997 report by Israel's Women's Network concluded that ROC controls the sex industry throughout the nation. And police in the United Arab Emirates state that Russian crime organizations are heavily engaged in local prostitution of trafficked women.

Intelligence gathered by the FBI and the Royal Canadian Mounted Police over the past decade reveals that ROC has been expanding into the lucrative American and Canadian sex markets by exporting Russian and Ukrainian women into the strip club, peep show, escort and massage parlor trade in North America. FBI headquarters in Washington, D.C., has amassed impressive dossiers showing that the Izmailovskaya, Dagestantsy, Solntsenskaya and Kazanskaya Russian crime syndicates have made inroads into the prostitution rackets throughout the country. Local ROC gangs in New York and New Jersey have even tried to muscle in on trafficking and prostitution activities run by other criminal organizations. In the summer of 1998, for example, crime boss Vyacheslav Ivankov—a.k.a. "the Red Godfather" and purported head of the Solntsevskaya syndicate operations in the U.S.—unleashed his goons in an effort to gain control of dance and modeling agencies that were importing trafficked Eastern European women for the flesh market. The FBI estimates that more than a dozen of these Russian-fronted dance and modeling agencies, each employing 60 to 200 East European women, supply women to the profusion of strip bars and peep shows run by the Italian Mafia in New York and New Jersey.

ROC, as well as a host of other Eastern European crime groups, is also expanding into Canada, particularly into

Toronto, Montreal and Vancouver. According to the 2002 Criminal Intelligence Service of Canada report on organized crime in Canada, "East European–based organized crime groups in Canada are well connected to criminal counterparts in Russia, Europe and the United States and function as integral parts of large-scale international organized crime networks." The CISC report notes that these crime groups are "known for their entrepreneurial and opportunistic tendencies, are quite adaptable and are strongly motivated by profit. As a result, they will engage in any type of criminal activity or attempt to penetrate any market sector they view as being vulnerable for exploitation," including prostitution.

Canadian and U.S. police intelligence reports also reveal that control of the trafficking trade in North America remains, for the most part, in the hands of smaller émigré gangs that are loosely connected to considerably more powerful organized crime syndicates abroad. As history shows, gangsters operating in foreign countries use their criminal connections in the motherland to prey on their own. This situation is no different. The majority of trafficking victims are recruited and sold by their own people.

The ROC, however, is not the only player by far. Enmeshed in the business are Ukrainian, Polish, Israeli, Czech, Georgian, Hungarian, Romanian, Bulgarian, Serbian and Albanian gangs, as well as the Italian Mafia, Chinese Triads and the Japanese Yakuza. International police reports from virtually every capital around the globe are replete with warnings about the involvement of these groups in the trafficking of women. Yet whatever the structure or the connections, the gangsters involved in the trade have two very powerful weapons at their disposal: an army of muscle to instill fear, and lots of money to influence and corrupt.

I WANTED TO FIND OUT just how difficult is it to purchase young Slavic women for the sex trade. It is, as I discovered, really quite easy. All that's needed is a connection and cold hard cash.

The meeting took place at an apartment in Ottawa, Canada's capital city, on a brisk, snowy night in early January 2003. I was a bit nervous. The man I was to meet was no ordinary low-level thug. Ludwig Fainberg is a notorious Israeli mobster with a hair-trigger temper and a penchant for extreme violence. According to FBI documents, he was the middleman for an international drugs and weapons smuggling conspiracy linking Colombian drug lords with the Russian Mafia in Miami. Fainberg's claim to fame was that in the mid-1990s, he ventured onto a high-security naval base in the far northern reaches of Russia. His mission was to negotiate the purchase of a Russian Cold War–era diesel submarine—complete with a retired naval captain and a twenty-five-man crew—for the Colombian cocaine cartel. The price tag: a cool $5.5 million. The vessel was to be used to smuggle tons of white powder along the California coast. The deal fell through.

From 1990 until he was arrested and charged in Miami in February 1997 for smuggling and racketeering, Fainberg ran an infamous strip club called Porky's. The pink neon club on the fringe of Miami International Airport was a magnet for Russian hoods and sleazy East European émigrés with misbegotten fortunes and visions of untapped criminal proceeds.

Fainberg's rise through ROC ranks is the stuff of Hollywood B-movies. He was born in Odessa, Ukraine, in 1958. When he was thirteen he and his parents immigrated to Israel. Later, he tried out for the Israeli Marines, wanting to become a Navy Seal. He flunked basic training. Then he wanted to become an officer in the Israeli Army but failed the exam. His over-inflated ego bruised, he decided to try his luck elsewhere. In 1980 he packed a suitcase and headed for Berlin, where he earned his stripes as a street-level goon in extortion and credit card fraud. Four years later he set out for the United States—a land he fondly refers to as "the Wild West because it is so easy to steal there!"

He settled in the Brighton Beach area of Brooklyn, which had become the seat of the Organizatsiya, as the Russian mob is often called. There he linked up with the mob and specialized in arson—torching businesses competing with those that were Russian owned. In 1990 he moved to Miami to run Porky's. Nine years later he was convicted on racketeering charges and sentenced to thirty-seven months in prison. Since he had already spent thirty months in jail awaiting trial, Fainberg was deported to Israel. The next year he turned up in Canada with dreams of making it rich in the flesh trade. Not long after his arrival he married a Canadian and moved into a comfortable apartment along the Ottawa River with his new bride and his ten-year-old daughter from a previous marriage.

I entered the well-appointed two-bedroom flat and Fainberg stared hard into my face as we shook hands. He's a burly man with a thin goatee and short-cropped hair, and he was clearly sizing me up. I must have passed. He gripped my hand firmly and escorted me to the living room, which was outfitted with the latest gizmos in video and audio entertainment. I sank down into a soft, black kid-leather couch while he retreated to the kitchen to get a couple of imported beers.

"You can call me Tarzan," he began as he burst back into the room. With a proud boyish grin, he tossed me one of his business cards. The cover of the custom-made two-fold card sported the caricature of a mop-topped muscular man under the name Porky's. The inside featured a cartoon of an ample nude woman bending over in knee-high, stiletto-heeled boots. Underneath was his name—"Tarzan Da Boss"—and on the opposite side "Welcome to Planet Sex, Land of Fantasy." According to Fainberg, he was nicknamed Tarzan because he once sported a wild mane of hair and acted as though he was straight out of a jungle. These days, for travel and immigration purposes, he's known as Alon Bar. The former strip-club owner legally changed his name during his last pit stop in Israel.

The man is a consummate braggart. For the better part of the evening he crowed about his illicit escapades and nefarious underworld connections and boasted that his life would make a spectacular Hollywood movie. He even talked about penning his memoirs. "It would be number one on the *New York Times* bestseller list." But there's one aspect of his life he probably wouldn't want revealed in any book. Fainberg relishes putting women in their place. In one violent incident in Miami, undercover agents with the FBI and U.S. Drug Enforcement Agency watched from a safe distance as he chased a stripper out of Porky's and slammed her head repeatedly against the door of his Mercedes until the car was covered with blood. In another episode, he beat a dancer in the parking lot outside the club and then made her eat gravel. Clearly he was no gentleman, and every woman in his club knew it. Incredibly, he attributes this mean streak to his upbringing: "In Russia, it's quite normal for men to slap women. It is cultural. It is part of life."

Fainberg prefers to see himself as an astute businessman, and if there's a business he firmly grasps, it's the flesh trade. "It can make you a millionaire in no time," he said, winking. His Canadian dream was to open a strip club in Gatineau, Quebec. The club, across the bridge from the nation's capital, would feature imported talent—Russian and Ukrainian strippers and lap dancers. When I met with him he was shopping for a Canadian partner and trolling for an infusion of cash. I asked Tarzan what he would bring to the deal. He recited his know-how and his unique expertise in importing entertainment.

After an hour I shifted the conversation to the issue at hand: buying women. With an earnest, businesslike expression, Fainberg said flat-out that it was an easy feat—he could bring women in from Russia, Ukraine, Romania or the Czech Republic. "No problem. The price is $10,000 with the girl landed. It is simple. It is easy to get access to the girls. It's a phone call. I know the brokers in Moscow, St. Petersburg and Kyiv. I can call Moscow tomorrow and show you how easy it is. I can get ten to fifteen to twenty girls shipped to me in a week." Clearly, he had done this many times before.

"They know exactly what they're being hired to do?" I asked. "They're not being forced?"

"They know why they are coming and what they are going to do. They will not be any trouble," he assured me.

Guardedly I mentioned that while surfing the internet, I had tripped on FBI and U.S. State Department documents that said he "likely trafficked in women." That got his attention. As he shifted to the edge of his seat, Fainberg's eyes flashed in indignation. "That is bullshit. I never trafficked in women. I don't need trafficked women. Agents in Russia are overwhelmed with women who want to do this voluntarily. If you look at their living conditions in Russia, there is no way of surviving. They live in poverty. At least this way, they can make a living. When people need to eat, what are you going to do?"

"Given what you've just said, they're not really prostitutes," I interjected.

Fainberg paused for a moment, mulling over my words. Then with a laugh, he shot back: "My opinion is a prostitute is someone who is selling herself. From that point of view that is what they are. It is true they definitely do not want to do this. They are being pushed by their social level of their life. They're getting pushed by necessity. They're being pushed to survive. Then maybe they're not really prostitutes."

He even held himself out as a Good Samaritan: "The girls come here and they send some money home and the family lives. If they don't come to work here or in Germany or England, their family suffers. I give the girls a chance to earn money. For me, it is a business transaction, plain and simple, but I am also helping these women out."

"I've heard that a lot of these women have no idea they're going into prostitution when they accept these so-called job offers to work abroad," I countered. "In fact, I've read that a lot of them think they're going to be waitresses or hotel cleaning staff."

Fainberg held his fire.

I find that difficult to believe. I was present on many occasions when girls were being hired. Plus, at some point I had over twenty girls from Russia, Ukraine and Romania who came to work in the States. Maybe some of them don't know. But how stupid do you have to be that you are going to a different country to work as a waitress or dancer in a club? It is really stupidity. It's dumb. Women know what they are going for. Sometimes when they realize their mistakes or they're getting hurt, it's easy to blame somebody else for being so dumb. I think they should only blame themselves for getting into that.

He grudgingly conceded that some of these women are duped. "I think 10 percent don't know what they're getting into. Ninety percent know exactly what they're going to do. What they may not know exactly is the conditions or how much money they will get."

"You don't have a problem with pushing women who are absolutely destitute into prostitution?"

"Look, that's what they can offer. Life is a business. It's a trade. You want to give something for nothing? You can help once or twice. But then ten, twenty or forty times? For that you want to get something in return."

"What kind of money are we talking here?" I asked. "How much will it cost to bring a woman over, and what kind of profit can be made?"

"If it is run the proper way, the clean way, you can have a good clientele and make a lot of money. You can buy a woman for $10,000 and you can make your money back in a week if she is pretty and she is young. Then everything else is profit."

I asked about getting the women into Canada or the United States.

"It is so simple, so very simple," he bragged. "You know after 9/11 how difficult it was supposed to be to get into the United States? I will show you right now how easily we can get into the United States and then come back, and nobody will ever know we were in there." He went on to hint that certain Russian mobsters have connections with Native gangs whose reserves straddle the Canada–U.S. border.

A couple of days later, Canadian Immigration authorities swooped in and arrested Fainberg in his comfortable Ottawa lair. He was labeled a threat to national security and public safety, and ordered deported to Israel.

THE EASE WITH WHICH criminals like Fainberg enter the flesh trade is not only sobering; it's absolutely astounding. Take the classic trafficking case in Chicago that began in September 1996.

Alex Mishulovich, a thirty-eight-year-old unemployed insurance broker, was approached by Serguie Tcharouchine, a

Russian cab driver, with a no-lose, moneymaking business proposition: fly to Riga, the capital of Latvia, to recruit beautiful young women as nude dancers for local strip clubs in the Windy City. Serguie had a silent partner willing to put up the cash. Mishulovich was the ideal front man because he was a newly minted U.S. citizen and could travel freely to the former Soviet Union. He was also the perfect person to manage the women once they were in the States, largely because of his persona: he was a thug. It didn't take much convincing, and a month later he set off for Riga.

Mishulovich was no fool. He knew he needed help with the sales pitch; his demeanor was a little too intimidating. He was heavy-set, wore thick black-plastic-rimmed glasses, sported a goatee and had a shaved head. Soon after his arrival he hooked up with an obliging associate—a twenty-one-year-old leggy blue-eyed blonde named Rudite Pede. After cementing the deal, the duo set off to troll the streets for pretty women.

Rudite was the perfect lure, introducing her conquests to her "American businessman" partner. Passing himself off as the owner of a sophisticated, exclusive "gentlemen's club," Mishulovich said he was looking to hire dancers for his Chicago establishment. He stressed that no sex, no nudity and no touching was permitted. His dancers danced in a bikini, he assured the dubious women, never topless or nude, and they made $60,000 a year. In Latvia, where the average monthly income is about $250, the offer was just too enticing to turn down. In no time at all the pair had reeled in five young hopefuls: all in their early twenties, all blondes and all striking.

There was a bit of a twist in getting the girls into the States. Mishulovich claimed he had a connection at the U.S. embassy in Riga, which made it easier for him to get tourist visas. He coached the girls on what to say to the official and helped them fill out their visa applications. But as the departure date neared, one of the women got cold feet. She felt that something wasn't quite right and tried to pull out. Mishulovich went berserk. Screaming like a madman, he pulled her aside and threatened to cut up her "pretty face" so that no man would ever want to look at her again. He also warned her that he had many friends in the feared Chechen Mafia, a notorious crime organization, who would be "happy" to kill her family. The terrified woman duly boarded the plane bound for the U.S.

Upon arriving at Chicago's O'Hare airport the girls were picked up by Serguie, who relieved them of their travel documents and return airline tickets. They were taken to the Mount Prospect suburb, where they were locked in a one-bedroom apartment. Serguie became their constant guard. Once on American soil, Mishulovich informed the women that they each owed him $60,000 for the airline tickets and arrangements to enter the U.S. They would have to pay off their debt by dancing nude in a strip bar. When one of the girls flat-out refused, he slammed her head into a wall. The woman sustained a concussion and was left bedridden for days. Worried about raising suspicions, her new owner refused to take her to a hospital or call in a doctor. Another woman who balked was hit in the head with Rollerblades, given a black eye and punched in the nose.

Throughout their ordeal the women were governed by strict rules enforced by verbal tirades and random beatings. They couldn't leave the apartment without Serguie in tow. When he left his post he locked them in and took away the phone. But Mishulovich was the real enforcer. He swaggered around the apartment toting a rifle and a pistol. When the girls talked back or didn't make enough money on a given night, he took them to the garage and brutally beat them.

On one occasion, when the girls were preparing dinner, he grabbed one of them, put a gun to her head and boasted how easy it would be to pull the trigger. On another, he put a knife to a woman's throat, threatening to slash her face. He repeatedly warned them that if they happened to get themselves arrested and deported to their homeland, he would track them down and would enlist the help of his Chechen Mafia connections in Riga to rape and kill them and their families. To emphasize his point, from the neck of one of the girls he snapped a locket that contained a picture of her mother, bellowing that now it would be easier for his mob associates to hunt the woman down and kill her if the need arose.

Mishulovich was also a consummate pig. He constantly made crude advances. He would paw the women, masturbate in front of them, watch pornographic videos when they were around and barge into the washroom when they were showering and demand that they perform oral sex on him.

Within a couple of weeks he managed to get them all California driver's licenses and fake social security cards. Then he drove the girls to an audition at a local strip club, presenting them as experienced dancers with expertise in Florida and the Windy City. But the club manager could see that these women were pathetically inept at exotic dance, and they were shown the door. Mishulovich exploded in rage. He dispatched Serguie to the local video outlet to rent the movies *Striptease,* starring Demi Moore, and *Showgirls,* starring Elizabeth Berkley. The girls were forced to watch them over and over, while practicing bump-and-grind techniques in the living room under the watchful eyes of their controllers.

Once they had their dance routines down pat they were farmed out to local strip bars—the Skybox, the Crazy Horse and the Admiral Theatre . . . and the money came rolling in. Every evening Mishulovich or Serguie drove them to work, picked them up afterward and collected the cash. Each girl brought in $200 to $500 a night. Mishulovich took virtually all their earnings, leaving them with no more than $20 a day. He also went through their purses and threatened to strip-search them if he suspected they were hiding cash. He then split the proceeds with his partner. Times were good.

In no time at all, Mishulovich elevated his status in Chicago's Russian-Jewish émigré community and in the process became a big spender, fond of untold luxuries and the finer things in life. He shopped at upscale shops, wore designer suits, dined at exclusive restaurants and drank expensive liquor.

Then came the first sign of trouble. In January 1997 Serguie was nabbed while shoplifting at a Mount Prospect jewelry store. He was convicted, and since he didn't have permanent resident status in the U.S. he was deported to

Russia two months later. With Serguie out of the picture Mishulovich found himself visited by what had, until now, remained his silent partner—a twenty-something, bookish-looking man, wearing small wire-rimmed glasses. He had short, curly dark hair and a baby face. Formerly Vadim Gorokhovski, he now went by the name of Vadim Gorr, and he wanted to protect his investment.

Gorr and Mishulovich continued farming the girls out and raking in the cash—day in, day out. But by early summer the duo got worried that U.S. immigration authorities might stumble across their scheme. Reluctantly, they decided to release the girls. Three of them immediately returned to Latvia. The other two remained in the U.S., hooking up with love-struck clients.

But Gorr and Mishulovich knew they had latched on to a good thing and didn't want to let it go. And so in November 1997 they flew to Minsk intending to recruit a second batch of women. This time, however, their ruse slammed into a brick wall when an astute visa officer at the American embassy smelled a rat and summarily rejected the women's applications.

Back in Latvia, the official at the American embassy in Riga who had cleared the original tourist visas for the Latvian women ran into one of the girls soon after she had returned home. The young woman relayed her incredible story. Enraged, the officer filed a full report with the U.S. State Department, and the matter was passed on to the FBI.

The case was assigned to special agent Michael Brown, a six-foot-two, 225-pound detective straight out of central casting. The agent, who had been working on the Eastern European Crime Squad, immediately ran a trace on Mishulovich and Gorr. The trace showed that both men, now naturalized American citizens, had emigrated from Russia in the early 1980s with their parents.

"They came at the time there was a huge influx of Russian Jews into the United States," Brown said. "Both families sought and obtained refugee status, claiming they were persecuted by the Soviets because they were Jewish."

With the evidence in place, the partners were picked up and charged in September 1998. Following their arrest, Gorr "lawyered up" and kept his mouth shut. Mishulovich was another story. He just kept yapping.

"I talked to him at length," Brown recounted. "He's a very intelligent, well-spoken man. There's no doubt about it. He was not an idiot. I deal with mostly gangs and drugs and uneducated and ignorant people. His English was phenomenal. But if you look at the facts, well, he's one repugnant person."

What bothered him most was that Mishulovich wasn't the least bit remorseful about the way he had treated the women. "If anything, he acted like he's almost aristocracy. He'd say 'They're scum. They're peasants. Spit on them. Don't take their word for anything. They're Baltic whores.' That was the term he used to describe them."

Mishulovich was a manipulative sleaze to the very end, hoping his cooperation would net him a lower jail sentence. Clearly, his objective was to foist the brunt of the blame on

Gorr, who he maintained was the brains behind the entire operation. Gorr, meanwhile, planned to paint himself as a naive bit player.

According to Brown,

> One of my theories on this is that Gorr was a very clever and calculating man and that he needed a fall guy or a front man, so that if anything ever did blow up, someone else would take the heat for it. That's why he recruited Serguie, who in turn found Mishulovich. They needed somebody to go out to Riga and recruit the girls. Somebody to sign their name on the visa applications as to being the sponsor for the girls. Somebody's house where the girls had to stay. Somebody to interact with them and take them to and from the clubs. Somebody to keep them in line if they got out of line. Somebody to do the dirty work.
>
> Mishulovich was that somebody, and the only reason that Gorr stepped up is because Serguie got deported and he wasn't gonna get any more of the money unless he had direct contact with Mishulovich.

The FBI's case rested largely on the shoulders of one key prosecution witness—the twenty-two-year-old Latvian woman who had recounted her story to the U.S. embassy official in Riga. As Brown recalled,

> She had guts. She had courage. If we didn't have her testimony, the case never would have gone forward. This gal has had a lot of problems as a result of all this too. There was a lot of psychological trauma associated with all of this because

she was beaten and abused. There were suicide attempts. It took me an awful long time to have her admit that there were sexual assaults that took place throughout the ordeal.

Brown said he interviewed all the girls. A couple of them decided not to cooperate. "There were a lot of reasons—fear for their families back home, distrust of law enforcement. Be mindful of the climate over there. It's a former Soviet state, and there's a high level of corruption over there. They equate the FBI with the KGB [the much-feared former Soviet secret police]."

After a ten-day trial in December 1999, the jury found Gorr guilty on four counts of visa fraud for helping to get the Latvian women into the U.S. under false pretenses. Wiping tears from his eyes, a jubilant Gorr hugged his attorney. He was acquitted of the far more serious charges of forcing the women into involuntary servitude. In late December 2001, the twenty-nine-year-old was sentenced to three years in prison and fined a measly $5000.

On February 13, 2002, Mishulovich stood before a judge for sentencing. He read a fifteen-minute statement, claiming that while he was guilty of being involved in "a horrible, disgusting, stupid business," it was Gorr, not he, who had been the brains behind the scheme. The former "businessman" begged for "a second chance." The court didn't buy it. Having pled guilty to a raft of charges, including involuntary servitude and conspiracy to defraud the United States, he was sentenced to 112 months in the penitentiary.

THE CHICAGO CASE is a frightening example of just how easily low-life thugs can jump on the trafficking bandwagon. But it's not only gutter trash like Mishulovich and Gorr who leech off naive and innocent women. The shocking arrest of a London doctor in 1999 showed just how widespread the trade has really become.

In 1994 Oksana Ryniekska graduated from medical school in Ukraine. At twenty-six, she soon realized that her life as a doctor in her native land didn't offer the money or lifestyle she wanted and felt she was entitled to. She opted to leave and headed for England. But soon after her arrival the silver lining turned to lead. The money just wasn't rolling in, and so she devised a plan to make handfuls of quick and easy cash. The newly minted doctor set up not a clinic but a brothel over a London dry-cleaning shop. For staff, she turned to the young women of her homeland, importing nine of them to work for her. Ryniekska told the women that she would help them obtain visas in order to enable them to study English. The only English they learned, however, was the sexual terminology required to understand and service their steady stream of clients. Needless to say, the money came rolling in, both from "in service" and from "home visits." In only eight months, before being busted in an undercover sting, Ryniekska had raked in more than $210,000.

At her trial in London in September 1999, the repentant doctor told the judge she felt "deeply ashamed." The judge was appalled at what Ryniekska had sunk to, calling it "nothing short of outrageous." The scam, the judge said, was particularly offensive given that she was a qualified medical doctor.

Nonetheless, Ryniekska was sentenced to a mere three months in prison, with a recommendation for deportation immediately upon release.

THE MASSIVE PROFITS from trafficking women into prostitution have also attracted gangs such as the Hell's Angels in Hamburg, Germany. In January 1999 the Hamburg biker chapter moved heavily into the prostitution racket. In no time it controlled more than 200 East European women in twenty-six brothels and "hour hotels" in the port city's Sankt Pauli red-light district, as well as two popular Hamburg strip clubs called Pascha and Eros. Their enterprise, however, was uncharacteristically short-lived. Seven members of the gang were arrested in a well-orchestrated sting operation in early November 2000.

According to the 529-page indictment, the bikers trafficked hundreds of Eastern European women into Germany to work as prostitutes in their brothels and fleabag hotels. The women were in the country illegally, were regularly abused and were forced to service clients seven days a week. The operation turned out to be incredibly successful. In the raid police had seized $350,000 in cash, a Lamborghini Diablo, three luxury Mercedes, five other high-end vehicles, a dozen customized Harley-Davidson motorcycles, several handguns and a grenade. The property was recovered from the posh Hamburg district of Elbchaussee from a supposed car mechanic, a photographer, a heating engineer, an electrician and a salesman. Based on the evidence, German police estimated that the bikers' sex proceeds totaled $17 million.

The bikers were charged with people smuggling, assault causing grievous bodily harm, pimping, blackmail and violent extortion. Their trial began in early August 2001 and was expected to last at least two years. Then, a half-day into the proceedings, echoes began to ricochet in the courthouse corridors that a plea bargain had been reached between the prosecution and the Angels' high-priced legal team. Two months later the accused gathered in court for sentencing, having pled guilty to a raft of charges. Despite the sheer gravity of the offenses, the bikers received anywhere from one year and four months to four years and eight months—an undeniable coup for the defense team. One biker's sixteen-month sentence was suspended because the court felt his chances of "reintegrating into society" were high. The gang members were also ordered to pay $5.5 million in fines. Later that day, out on the steps of the courthouse, the biker whose sentence was suspended beamed at the spectators, describing the judgment as "marvelous."

LIKE MOST CRIMINAL ENTERPRISES, trafficking in women for prostitution has become increasingly territorial. Any infringement on ROC's turf, for example, is met with swift retribution. ROC syndicates have been known to kill at the slightest hint of trouble. The trade is also resulting in an escalation of unprecedented violence against potential competitors and trafficked women alike. Albanian gangs are particularly notorious for their cruelty, terrorizing and torturing their victims and killing uncooperative girls. In some cases, gangs tattoo their "property" the way cowboys brand their cattle. The Yakuza in Japan have murdered women attempting to escape. The Turkish Mafia and Serbian gangsters have thrown girls from high-rise balconies for refusing to comply.

And when these gangs do kill, they often do it to send a message—as was the case in a brutal double murder that occurred in the Siberian city of Vladivostok on June 24, 1994.

When Natalie Samosalova walked by, heads turned in Vladivostok. The statuesque nineteen-year-old had tumbling blond hair and bedazzling azure blue eyes. In the summer of 1993 she got what she thought was an amazing break—her first opportunity to travel abroad. She was recruited to work as a dancer at the Skylight Disco in the gambling resort of Macau. Her application was expedited by an employment agency—the Society of Support to the Enterprises of Macau. Before she knew it, she found herself with another woman on a long train ride through China. When she finally arrived in Hong Kong she was met by a man called Valhiev. Natalie couldn't help noticing the jagged scar bisecting the man's face.

Valhiev, it turned out, was a Russian gangster with a reputation as "the most notorious pimp in Macau." In fact, he was one of ten known Russian pimps registered with the Macau government as working in local nightclubs as "pianists." It was safe to assume that none of them could strike a chord. Valhiev escorted the new arrivals to a flat shared by several other Russian women and explained in no uncertain terms what was expected of them. Dancing in nightclubs was not an option unless it was with a paying client. The next day Natalie was taken to a government office, where she was issued an identity card and a six-month work visa. That evening, she joined the ranks of 120 Russian women, most from Vladivostok, working in the enclave as call girls.

Natalie was extremely popular with high-spending clients and fetched a spectacular fee—$1000 to $3000 a night. The Russian gang that controlled her quickly realized her worth. She was a valuable asset, raking in a cool $55,000 a month. In April 1994 she met Gary Alderdice, a dashing lawyer from New Zealand who was renowned for defending members of the Hong Kong Triads. Alderdice was instantly smitten. It was a scene right out of *Pretty Woman,* except in this case the heroine belonged to the mob.

After a month-long sex-fest (which cost Alderdice $48,000), he professed his love to the glamorous hooker and she decided she wanted to be his. The haughty Natalie told Valhiev she wanted out. Skylight management complied, swiftly withdrawing its support for her visa. Her visa and work permit were summarily revoked, and the very next day Natalie found herself on a plane heading home.

Distraught, she phoned her lover in a panic. Alderdice promised to get her back. In late June he flew to Vladivostok, purportedly with a briefcase containing $150,000 in cash to negotiate her freedom from the mob. Natalie met him at the airport and they headed for her flat. They climbed three flights of stairs to her apartment and she ushered him in.

The very next day, Natalie's mother dropped by her daughter's apartment. When Natalie didn't answer, she knocked louder and harder. Again, nothing stirred. The woman enlisted the help of a neighbor and together they forced open the door. Lying in the hallway was the blood-soaked corpse of a man. He had been shot in the eye at what was clearly close range. In the living room Natalie lay stretched out on the floor, hands tied behind her back with a rope. She too had been shot in the head.

Earlier that morning, at about three-thirty, the neighbor who helped open the door had been jolted out of sleep by noises coming from Natalie's flat. She couldn't put her finger on it but it reminded her, she said, of the sound of "people chopping wood." The neighbor called the police, but her concerns were summarily dismissed. She was told to call back "if something serious happens."

The ensuing investigation was anything but thorough. Police quickly labeled it a "robbery," hoping to close the case. The prosecutor's initial hunch was that Alderdice was simply in the wrong place at the wrong time. Vladivostok, after all, is a naval port, a city known as the "Wild East" where crime and corruption are known to run deep. The prosecutor figured a couple of two-bit thugs saw the dashing, well-dressed lawyer, assumed he was carrying cash and followed him into the decrepit building. But the facts didn't add up. There was no forced entry. Natalie had been clearly tortured. And the murders were carried out execution-style. From what the investigators were able to piece together, the couple arrived at the apartment but didn't stay very long. According to the neighbor across the hall, they left a short while later and returned again around 11 p.m. There were at least two other men in tow. The rest remains hazy, but for Alderdice's friends and colleagues back home, the motive is clear.

"I know how the Russian vice operators work," says long-time friend Mike Prew, who is also a former chief of Interpol in Hong Kong. "They're the worst. Once the girls get involved in the syndicates, they don't get out or they get murdered." Prew firmly believes the Russian Mafia was behind the slayings and that the couple were victims of a deliberate and professional gangland execution. The message was simple: this is what you can expect if you leave. No doubt it rang loud and clear for the girls still working in Macau. They snapped back into line.

CLICK OF A
MOUSE

Business has tripled with the internet.

—A WEALTHY BROTHEL OWNER/TRAFFICKER IN TEL AVIV

THE MASSIVE WORLDWIDE RECRUITMENT of women into the flesh trade is fueled by one factor alone—the global demand for purchased sex by men. Tomes have been written about prostitutes and prostitution, largely because many women have been willing to speak out. By comparison, the legions of men who use these women nightly have managed to escape the microscope. As a group they remain largely unstudied; unsurprisingly, they keep their exploits to themselves. But while comparatively little is known about the men who frequent prostitutes, those in the front lines—from pimps to NGO workers—here offer their views. And the thoughts of the men themselves, as expressed on the burgeoning websites that offer women for sale, provide their own chilling perspective.

IN TEL AVIV'S OLD BUS STATION DISTRICT, strings of twinkling Christmas mini-lights beckon from signs bent in the shape of hearts and cherubs toting bows and arrows. But a closer examination of the area reveals that there is nothing festive or romantic about what these lights advertise. The place is awash in pitiful brothels, and business is brisk as platoons of men prowl the narrow side streets for a moment of passion. Behind tattered red curtains hanging from doorways, bleached blondes and tawny brunettes dressed in low-cut T-shirts and spandex scrunch together on sofas in clumps of four, five or six, waiting for the next client. They puff anxiously on cigarettes while perspiring men of all ages, shapes and sizes idle in the doorways ogling the merchandise.

At a ramshackle brothel, a pimp slouches behind a small metal desk wiping beads of sweat off his brow with a cheap handkerchief. His head is shaved and his pockmarked face sports a three-day stubble. An overweight, middle-aged man, who had been pacing furtively up and down the strip, peers in. The pimp shoots a look at the doorway and eagerly beckons him into the room.

"Enter! Enter! Take the one with the brown hair," he calls out with a wide, pasted-on grin. "She likes you. You won't be disappointed. Come! Come!"

The woman, who looks about twenty, propels herself up from a stained, pale green crushed-velvet couch and scurries toward the man before he can have a second thought. With a forced smile, she grabs his hand and pulls him into a back room. Fifteen minutes later he scoots out, looking sheepish, weak-kneed and fifty shekels lighter.

It's mid-afternoon outside a brothel and there's a lull in the traffic. David, a bear of a man with a buzz cut and one continuous bushy eyebrow, is standing outside his dingy establishment puffing on a cigarette. He's a gregarious sort who enjoys meeting and chatting with foreigners about politics, economics and sex. David sees himself as something of an urban sociologist and, if anything, he's definitely a front-line observer of a particular brand of humanity.

"All types of men come here," David booms in a baritone voice.

Married, single, soldiers, businessmen and the religious. I read in a Tel Aviv newspaper that a million men a month in Israel visit a prostitute. There is nothing wrong in this. A man needs release and there is nothing immoral in that. It is not about cheating. It is simply about release. A lot of single men go for necessity. A lot of men are insecure. They cannot get girls. You're a good-looking guy. I'm a good-looking guy. We can get women without having to pay. A lot of men cannot. They're shy or they may have a physical problem, a mental problem or a medical problem. They can be fat and ugly or not the right age. They cannot simply go out and meet a woman. Many men also come here because it is a well-known fact in Israel that Jewish women do not like to do certain things. The men know they can get that here. For them prostitution is their savior.

"And you're the delivery man?"

"I am the middleman," he said with a proud grin.

Look, men need women. It is natural. When I was a kid growing up in Russia, my father took me to a farm. He pointed to one field. It was full of cows. More than two dozen! Then my father took me to another field where there was one bull. One bull to service all these cows! He told me it is because a bull needs more than one cow! It is the same with men. This is our genetics. It is the way we are. It doesn't make us bad or make us pigs. It is a proven fact men need more sexual activity than a woman. So what do you do?

David is on a roll and there is no stopping him.

With prostitution you have no rapes. You bring in these women and innocent girls are not raped. That is why I believe in prostitution and would very much like to see it legalized everywhere. I believe because of it a lot of rapes are prevented. Men, because of the way we are built, our sexual will, our potential, our necessity, we need to do this. We need sex.

While he blathers on about the important service he provides for his brothers, there are many people in Israel who are deeply disturbed by what's happening on the side streets and back alleys of their country. In a modest apartment in a comfortable section of Tel Aviv, far from the red-light district, Leah Gruenpeter-Gold and Nissan Ben-Ami shake their heads in disgust at the opening of so many bordellos and the wholesale trafficking of young Natashas. Leah and Nissan are co-directors of the Awareness Center—a nongovernmental group that specializes in research on trafficking in women and prostitution in Israel.

"Israeli men have simply grown used to the idea that women can be bought," Gruenpeter-Gold began. "Both married and single men no longer want to work at relationships. For them it is easier to purchase sex when they want it."

"On the Jewish New Year, I went down to the old bus station area to see what was happening," Ben-Ami recalled. "There were young men queuing up in the streets outside each brothel. When you look into the reception area you could see all these sad and upset women, and when they see you, they suddenly look up and smile. They are happy to see you because they have to be happy or else."

What particularly offends Ben-Ami is the *haredim* (orthodox Jews) who crowd the Tel Aviv brothels on Friday mornings and afternoons for a pre-Shabbat tumble.

> When you go to the area of the Stock Exchange or the Diamond Exchange, you see a lot of prostitution and a lot of very, very religious men—because these men need sex but the women in their society cannot give it to them when they want it. They also cannot masturbate because they cannot waste their sperm. So they have to do it with a woman. These men also do not use condoms, therefore they must pay the pimps more. So in order to satisfy the needs of these men, we have to sacrifice these women.

"Because these women are not human beings," Gruenpeter-Gold said indignantly. "They are foreign women. The religious prefer it to be with foreign women because then they don't wrong Jewish women."

"Yet officially," Ben-Ami said, "the religious are very much against trafficking and prostitution. So, on one hand, many religious are against these brothels and, on the other hand, they need sex."

"It is all very hypocritical," Gruenpeter-Gold added.

ONE WAY TO GET A FIRST-HAND GLIMPSE into the mindset of the secret order of prostitute users is to eavesdrop on their internet musings. A good place to start is the World Sex Guide, which boasts almost 6000 members. The discussion board shows just how deluded most of these men are. Many brag about their lovemaking prowess in pornographic detail, holding themselves out as superstuds because the women they buy writhe, climb the walls and moan in sheer ecstasy at their every thrust. But more disconcerting is their unwavering belief that their right to sex overrides the rights of the women and girls they're using. For these men it's all about their needs, and how they satisfy them is their business. Throughout the website postings are endless rationalizations for why they do it. They blame their wives for sexually unfulfilling marriages. They blame women for not putting out after an expensive dinner date. And when these men don't measure up in the bedroom, guess who they blame? They also label all women as gold diggers and counter that hookers don't ask for flowers.

But the argument that rings out loudest is their "need" to have sex. In the minds of most of these men, sex is a biological imperative that must be satisfied; buying sex, therefore, is a natural activity. It's a perfectly logical alternative to an unfulfilling or nonexistent relationship. As long as they have the cash, they're *entitled* to satisfy their sexual urges—whatever they may be and whenever they strike. But there's no biological imperative I've ever heard of for men to have an orgasm any set number of times a day, week, month or year. While it may be unpleasant to go without sexual release for long periods, the absence of another person in the equation doesn't threaten a man's very survival. Nonetheless, voicing this "male sexual need," along with the common belief that prostitutes are dirty and impure, makes it easy for the johns to defend their actions. To them, prostitution is nothing more than a commodity exchange, and they're simply behaving as any other consumer would. Their bottom line is: if they don't purchase the service, the next man in line will, and the line is very, very long.

What's particularly worrisome about these website postings is how little thought is given to the so-called prostitutes they engage with. Most of these women are victims, forced into the vicious sex trap long before they reach the age of consent. Girls as young as ten, eleven and twelve are routinely found in brothels and on the streets worldwide. But in the johns' world, this means only that they're probably free of sexually transmitted diseases, especially HIV and AIDS.

While the reasons for frequenting prostitutes may vary from one man to the next, one thing remains clear: the world of prostitution is laden with hypocrisy and double standards. The women are called "prostitutes," "whores," "hookers," "sluts," "harlots"—terms laced with opprobrium and distaste. The men who use them go by gentler names—"patrons," "clients," "johns"—making them sound refined by comparison. This wordsmithing is not without purpose—it makes it easier for men and society to objectify, commodify and then dismiss the victims. For most people, prostitutes are nameless faces, social pariahs unworthy of compassion or understanding. The men who use them, on the other hand, are either sowing their wild oats or just being guys. They can even be viewed as valuable members of society—stressed-out CEOs, for example, who may occasionally dabble in questionable sexual behavior. And as long as they don a condom, who gets hurt?

Today, the hunt for cheap, easy prey has been made significantly easier because the prowlers know exactly where to click. Without a doubt, the internet has turned the already blistering global sex market into a red-hot inferno. Even a cursory scan of adult sex sites shows that the net has become the biggest whorehouse on the planet. Every day, hundreds of sites entice men around the world into virtual brothels where women and girls are bought and sold—sometimes even auctioned off—like livestock. The sites are high gloss, in your face and hard sell, telling buyers exactly what they'll get for their money. The merchandise is tempestuously arranged, with photos of leggy blondes and sultry-eyed redheads. There's something for everyone—virgins, brides, sex tours, online escort services, live interactive sex shows.

Name the permutation and it will be delivered. All it takes is the click of a mouse.

Men and their mice were clicking heatedly on one particular site in early March 2002. The Ukrainian Exotic Escort Agency in Odessa was taking its cue from eBay and holding an auction. But this was no ordinary auction. The commodity was a nineteen-year-old virgin. The offering included a full package tour: visa, airfare and twenty-four hours with the girl. The bids opened at $1500, and by the end of the month they had a winner. On March 28 the outcome was posted: "Our congratulation to Mr. D____ from France! $3000 for Ukrainian virgin Diana." The unknown factor was whether Diana had been trafficked and coerced or if she was doing this of her own free will. After all, why would a nineteen-year-old virgin want to give herself to a complete stranger? Judging from the electrified hum on various adult websites, no one seemed the least bit concerned about the girl's situation. The lustful miscreants in the chat rooms thought only of what she looked like and whether she'd be worth it.

While the international flesh trade has flourished for decades, the internet is the match that has set the sex market ablaze. Recognizing the net's potency, in no time porn kings, pimps and traffickers were online promoting their products and services. Indeed, many observers believe that the net is singularly responsible for the incredible explosion in the trafficking of women and girls worldwide.

STANDING OUTSIDE A BROTHEL on a garbage-strewn side street near the old bus station in Tel Aviv, Lev lights up a cigarette. It's the middle of the afternoon and business is slow. I approach and strike up a conversation.

"Can I take a look?" I asked.

"Sure. I give you a special price," he said as he pulled back the faded red curtain dangling from the doorway.

Sitting on a couch were four young women. All looked drawn and unenthusiastic. The women were in various forms of undress. Not one was older than twenty-two.

"Where are they from?" I asked.

"Russia."

"They're all from Russia?"

"Russia, Ukraine, Moldova . . . what's the difference?"

"What's her name?" I asked, pointing to a slender, dark-haired, dark-eyed girl who looked about seventeen.

"Natasha. She is my favorite. She will not disappoint you."

"Let me think about it for a moment."

"No pressure. No pressure," Lev said with a smirk.

I looked over at his desk and noticed a computer. Beside it was a scanner and an ink-jet color printer.

"I see you've gone high tech," I said.

"Pentium 3. Very fast. I have my own website," Lev boasted. "Come, I will show you."

Lev opened Netscape, clicked Favorites on the tool bar menu and scrolled down to his personal setting. In a few moments his website popped up, displaying individual photographs of his girls—all lying naked on a cheesy cheetah-skin carpet. Not one smiled or offered up an inviting gaze. Looking into their faces, I could tell they were embarrassed.

"Do you get a lot of hits?"

"Every day. Dozens and dozens. Business has tripled with the internet. Customers see what I have to offer. They know the girl they will get and what she will do. I have had many visitors from America, Canada, Britain, Europe and some from Japan. They all found me on the internet. So what about you?"

"What about me?"

"Have you made up your mind?"

"Yeah. I'm not interested."

As I turned and left, I could hear Lev muttering what I figured were a few choice epithets in Hebrew. Walking toward my hotel, I wondered how those young women felt knowing online lechers far and wide were ogling their photographs. I also thought about Lev's comment: that the internet has tripled his business, and that men were flying in specifically to use his girls.

SCORES OF WEBSITES offer sex-craving men advice on where to get the most for their hard-earned dollar, and certainly one of the most popular online forums is the World Sex Guide. Its mission, it boasts, is simple: "Finding women and getting laid. If you feel offended by stuff like this, I don't care." Visitors and contributors to this site take questions about buying sex very seriously. The discussion board contains thousands of first-hand reports from every country in the world. "If you want to know where the action is in your town or at your next travel destination, this is where you get the answers," the site declares. "Knowledge is power, and reading up on the local scene before

you get there lets you hit the ground running while avoiding
the traps. Benefit from the observations of your fellow adven-
turers, and be sure to post your own experiences."

The World Sex Guide is a wellspring of information on
every prostitution-related topic under the sun. Testimonials
from satisfied customers, warnings from disillusioned johns and
advice on how to procure the best hookers in more than a
hundred countries around the globe pour forth. Every day,
legions of men, hungry for sex, swarm onto this and other
similar sites in their quest for flesh.

One online user, going by the name Travel Sexman, asked
for tips on where he could get the most bang for his buck:
"Which city has the best sex that's worth spending my euros—
Frankfurt or Prague or Amsterdam?" Less than an hour later, he
had a reply. "Amsterdam has the best classical red-light district
with girls in the windows, but is just there for tourists. Prague
is good, but not as cheap as you would think." The conclusion:
"All in all Frankfurt is the best."

The postings even offer up travel directions: "If you go to
Frankfurt and rent a car and head to Atlantis in Altenstadt or
Oase in Burgholzhausen you will find 40 to 60 completely
naked women in a very clean and pleasant atmosphere," the
Frankfurt booster wrote.

A typical exchange begins with a question about a city, like
this one from an American man traveling to Norway: "I will be
in Helsinki for business at the end of the month. What's the
action?" The rapid reply: "If you want to do 'Russia Lite'
Helsinki is a good starting point. Prices are higher than in some

parts of FSU [former Soviet Union] but in my experience $150 gets you a very attractive girl for the night."

A Canadian asked for advice on where to go during a stopover in Turkey: "Hi, I will have a summer layover of a day or two in Istanbul on my way to Ukraine. Any suggestions on where to go for some quick nookie? Eastern European quality would be ideal. Thanks!"

A couple of keystrokes later, he too had a response.

"Istanbul is a heaven for Ukrainian girls. And you're not limited to them at all. There are also Romanian, Russian, Bulgarian, Moldavian," a clearly satisfied visitor wrote. "If you go to Seranda in Istanbul you'll find loads of former USSR wenches and you can simply take them to the hotel right next door. It's not a rip-off either."

The sex industry has been a prime catalyst behind many of the major advances in computer technology since the net's inception, including privacy services, secure payment schemes and online database management. Pimps and pornographers have provided the impetus and cash for computer techno-wizards to come up with faster ways of delivering salacious products to an ever-expanding clientele.

Before the advent of the internet, a businessman traveling to Turkey would have been hard-pressed to find up-to-date reviews of Istanbul's escorts or hookers in the various underground sex magazines, much less get directions to actual sites and tips on which brothels provide the best and safest service. Now, with sites like the World Sex Guide, a stopover in this Byzantine metropolis can turn into an orgasmic yet cost-effective sexual smorgasbord.

The message boards are also chock-full of testosterone-laden bravado. Tinman from Wisconsin, for example, couldn't wait to tell his cybersex brothers about his recent sex tour to the Czech Republic:

> Prague is an awesome city yet almost strange. You're in one of the oldest and yet most beautiful cities in all of Europe during the day. And then at night it totally changes into an almost sex crazed city. You can find tons of strip clubs that offer a lot more than just shows for not all that much money. I went to one of these such clubs, which cost about $10U.S. to get in and then about $3U.S. for a pretty good beer. Meanwhile you could see some of the most beautiful women dance naked for you. In addition to the strippers, there are also a number of prostitutes that are sitting at different tables and couches waiting for you. If you happen to make eye contact with a few of them they will for the most part come on over to you and talk with you while feeling you up pretty good.
>
> One such girl came up to me and took me by the hand and led me to a couch with her and once seated began to kiss me quite heavily. She was absolutely beautiful and had an awesome looking body. After a few minutes of kissing she led me back to a hallway where for $50U.S. we could have a room for an hour. Once inside the room she sat me on the bed and began to perform a wonderful striptease for me and then began to undress me.

In pornographic detail, the Tinman went on about how he completely satisfied her with his male prowess. It was the most amazing time he ever had, he concluded, and through it all he never put on a condom.

One frequent contributor to the World Sex Guide is Cossem, a "senior member" of the discussion board who passes himself off as a lover of women and a connoisseur of sex. Cossem's topic of choice: hookers in the Holy Land. He points out that 98 percent of the prostitutes in Israel are Russian, but he doesn't differentiate between Russian, Ukrainian, Moldovan or Romanian. He also never reveals that many of them have been trafficked. After all, why spoil a fantasy with a chilling bucket of reality?

In a January 2003 posting, Cossem compared the local women with the Russians:

> Local pro talent does exist but they are practically all harden pros who despise men and hold there services in high value and are aloof from the Russian imports. But believe me some of the Russian imports are very good and a lot of them enjoy their work, get a lot of pleasure from it and it's the customers that gain. Mind you if you are young, good looking and have a easy way with women there is nothing stopping you picking up some real hot Israeli women for some of the greatest sex imaginable for free. But if you are an old pot bellied lecher don't bother trying. You will have to make do with the hundreds if not thousands of ex East Block girls who for a very small fee can make any man very happy for an hour or two.

Cossem's claim to fame is authoring the Tel Aviv Sex Report, a review of "the best health clubs (whorehouses) or Machonim in Hebrew." In it, he cites the Banana Club and

Club 101, where the going rate is 230 NIS (new Israeli shekels) for a half-hour. He gives the exchange rate: $1 US for 4.85 NIS. "So 230 will be about $47 US." He also recommends escort agencies "for much better value" and even posts the names of his favorite "hot girls." In one of his breathless reports, he writes about "a magnificent session" with what he calls "a perfect 10 in all aspects. Her name is Alina and she is a Russian import. She is tall, long blond natural hair, magnificent perfect body, beautiful eyes and face, nice boobs, erect and firm, also natural, plus a very friendly nature. Her performance was magnificent." He details his entire half-hour of pleasure before they "both collapsed on the bed sweating profusely even though the room was air conditioned," adding that he was 100 percent certain the woman's moans and groans were "all genuine." Cossem describes Alina as "really special." So special in fact that he posted the phone number of the agency and a website address showing her in the nude. "If anyone on this board is over this side of the world you should try her as you won't be sorry. I only hope she doesn't get over worked and ruined as this girl is a very rare gem and needs to be handled with care and respect."

Almost from the net's beginnings, sex tours to scores of countries around the globe have been a staple on adult websites. The operators make their money peddling packages lathered with promises of sexual nirvana. Typically, the tour sites don't offer sex outright but the advertising copy hints at what the escorts will do. They note that their girls are "open minded" and that they provide "full service" or the "girlfriend experience." The promises are interlaced with steamy catalogs of scantily clad women. Their physical attributes are prominent, along with lists of the sex acts that can be expected and details on the cost of the tour, airline tickets, hotel reservations and visa requirements.

The most popular tour destinations these days are the countries featuring women and girls from the former Soviet Union. The internet is teeming with sites promoting sex clubs, brothels, massage parlors and escort agencies in Frankfurt, London, Amsterdam, New York and Toronto. These sites also offer "romance" or "introduction" tours to St. Petersburg, Moscow, Minsk, Kyiv and Odessa. One of the more popular sex-tour agencies in Odessa declares, "We care about the needs of all our clients and want to make your staying here most enjoyable. We also pay attention to the health of our girls. Each girl passes through a full medical examination and analyses every week." The agency claims to put its girls through numerous "tests and erotic contests" to make them "really worthy" of the men they will service. The tour package includes being met at the airport, a room booked at a "fashionable" hotel, a driver, security, sightseeing excursions, restaurant reservations, visits to Russian bathhouses "and any other entertainment you wish." According to the site, "The main goal of our agency is to care about your comfort and need. You will not be bored with our girls."

The sex tours are flourishing for all sorts of reasons. Foremost, they give men a sense of freedom. By traveling to a foreign land for sex, they feel at liberty to do things they may never dare otherwise, whether because of community norms, family ties or, more to the point, criminal sanctions. The featured attraction for many of these men is the prospect of bedding a young girl, preferably a beautiful teenager. They know that if they were ever to try that at home, they'd find themselves behind bars. At home, no always means no. But when johns sign up for a tour, they know the girls are desperate and trained to please. In fact, the tour companies often guarantee their clients no regrets. The Odessa agency, for example, goes out of its way to suggest that its girls are up to the task: "Slavonic women have always been remarkable for their obedience and willingness to fulfill any wish. Time, spent with our girl, will stay in your mind and you will often remember it with satisfaction and pleasure."

For men who want more than just a one-night stand, the internet has also spawned a new generation of mail-order brides. Agencies and websites are marketing women from the former Soviet Union and developing countries as desirable mates for Western men. The sites are bursting with cookie-cutter bios and snapshots of attractive, fresh-faced, smiling women. The typical scenario involves male clients selecting up to a dozen women to "interview." Once they make their selection, the agents promptly arrange a seven- or fourteen-day tour to the woman's homeland. Judging from the price tag and the tour descriptions, marriage is the last thing on the minds of most of these men. The package offered, more often than not, is nothing more than a sex vacation extravaganza. And email-order brides aren't just the latest trend; they're a growing, multi-million-dollar business. The net is now the marketing tool of choice for so-called marriage agents worldwide, offering a faster and more cost-effective means to rotate the inventory and reach potential clients.

One site extols the attributes of Slavic brides, noting that Russian women "are much more patient" and tolerant than their Western counterparts. According to the site, "They are more considerate and dependable. They are partners, not competitors." It goes on to say that Russian women "have very low self-esteem," and that "while Western women think that they are goddesses and able to cope with anything on their own, a Russian woman will rarely leave a bad (really bad) husband because of the fear that she won't find another one. For many years the state and men have been oppressing them, and they don't think much about themselves." The offering concludes that Russian women are "well groomed, stylish and intelligent" and that "they are rarely overweight—probably, because of permanent stress and food that is expensive."

Russian women are particularly popular, as are women and girls from neighboring countries like Ukraine. The Russian International Marriage Agency, for example, marks itself out as having "the best girls and women" from the former Soviet Union. The agency's site begins by painting a tempting picture of romantic and family bliss: "Gentlemen, do you have dreams of a loving touch? Of a beautiful firm body in your bed? Of a happy child's laughter?" The last comment is particularly offensive. In the world of sex trafficking, it's a code—a signal to pedophiles that the offerings include girls. If the "gentleman" answers yes to the question, he's told, "You've found the right place!" And "Your dream can come true in a few minutes." The whole thing sounds pretty romantic until the reader gets to the part about the naked pictures: "Our ladies will not hide anything," the agency proclaims. "You will see them as they are—in the nude. Most of them have sets of photos. You will see everything you want to see. You won't ever be disappointed. We promise you won't be sorry."

These sites are simply fronts for buying and selling women. The first telltale clue is the erotic photographs. Surely a man in search of a wife would never make his selection from a nude catalog posted to the web! Furthermore, these agencies are not only issuing an invitation to sex; they're opening the door for women to be purchased and sold, not as potential wives but as virtual slaves. The agencies don't conduct any checks, nor do they screen any of the men who want to join. The only requirement is monetary: if the client pays the membership fee, he's in. This is not to say that some of these sites aren't legitimate. Some are. A lot of women do get marriage proposals and some end up with a husband who treats them right. But there are far too many tragic accounts of women being duped by men who offer them marriage only to traffic them into prostitution or turn them into their slaves in a far-off foreign land.

For those men who want excitement without the risk of travel or disease, the internet offers the ideal compromise: live interactive sex shows, or peep shows with a twist. Thanks to the latest in real-time communications and video-conferencing— yet more technologies developed by computer companies expressly for the porn industry—a voyeur in Miami can slip into a brothel in Minsk, order up a woman, sit back, undress and tell her how to move and how loud to moan. All from behind the shield of his computer terminal, a continent away! He watches her, but remains out of sight. The only thing she hears is his disembodied voice. Separated by thousands of kilometers, but connected through the net, they engage in a perverse game of Simon Says.

Bruce Taylor of the U.S. National Law Center for Children and Families considers these interactive sex shows as an extension of the trafficking problem. He notes that although law enforcement officials have long known that women and girls are forced into prostitution against their will, "now there is a new twist. The act can be sold around the world on the internet." According to Taylor, "People can get so selective that they can now see a particular type of woman doing a type of act." The problem, he stressed, is that over time, this will increase the demand for real sex slaves.

PORING OVER POSTINGS on the World Sex Guide, you find that most of the men sharing their steamy tales of their purchased conquest aren't the least bit interested in the dignity and rights of the women themselves. Post a comment about whether the women they use might have been forced into the trade and these lusty exploiters become downright incensed. Consider the debate sparked by Arab Man Observing when he pointed out that many of the so-called foreign prostitutes in the United Arab Emirates are nothing more than slaves. He wrote:

I'm a young Arabic man and I have been to Abu Dhabi and Dubai several times. Last time I was there for several weeks. I know the feeling when you get a working girl because I've done it myself. It starts as being fun and an enjoyable experience. The sex is probably the best you will ever get. But later when you hear the stories of some of these girls, it becomes very sad. A lot of those women come from Russia, Ukraine and Chechnya and have been trafficked to the country. Initially they did not know that they were going to work as prostitutes. They were promised decent jobs like a cashier or a waitress in a café.

He went on to describe how many of the women get trapped and what happens to them once they arrive in the UAE. "Those girls don't know anybody in the country, they don't have money to buy an airplane ticket back home, they don't trust their embassies to help them and they are scared to go to the police because the pimp manipulates them into believing that the police will arrest them and throw them in jail." What's worse, he noted, is that many of their families think they're working abroad for a respectable firm and saving money.

What is she going to tell them? That she left her country as a decent woman and came back after prostituting herself for months? That she was being sexually, physically and mentally abused by her pimp and by some of her customers? I know this for a fact as I saw marks of abuse on their bodies. I don't know what I would do in a situation like this but I let you think about it.

Then came the replies. One of the sharpest was from Fenster:

> Hey Arabic Man Observing, So what's your point, huh? You wanna be a social worker go work for www.gov. This is a board for men who wanna get laid, not for those who wanna hear slash wrist, sad violin stories. You seem to be big on passing blame and low on accountability. These women know fully well what they're doing and they chose to do it. Would your sister do it if she was poor and destitute? No. Why? Cause of her family values, she made a choice not to, and the others chose to sell themselves, they're responsible for their choices, enda story.

A similar tempest erupted when a man called Hunter recounted his trip to the Czech Republic: "I took a little trip to Dubi/Teblice in June. The two villages are close by and the easiest way to find them is to drive towards Dresden from Prague on motorway E-55. Dubi is closest to the German border and is full of bars with dancing girls, some very good looking, not many over 25, price range is about 50 DM for half an hour." The account droned on and on.

Hunter's review prompted a scathing reprimand from Anonymous: "Do you assholes know how many of those girls in that particular location are basically sex slaves who have been kidnapped from Russia, Ukraine, Belarus, etc.? What if that was your sister being forced to [service] 10 to 20 assholes like you a day?"

Hunter fired back. "What can I say, it's a dirty business, if you don't like to read about it I suggest you skip this site. I have a hard time seeing you changing anything by whining at the posters."

Coming to Hunter's defense, another online regular crowed: "These chicks are poor and I'm helping feed their family."

His assessment prompted a stinging rebuke from a woman who happened to be checking out the forum:

> Idiots. If you keep thinking that these women you are paying for sex are not victims, you thought wrong. They don't want to take their clothes off and sleep with some stranger who they are most likely not even attracted to. They feel degraded, nasty, sick by it, but they continue to do it, because they don't have any other skills and someone will beat their ass if they don't bring money. All of them are in dire need for help and prostitution is their last resort. If you want to help them, donate your money without trading for sex.

Then the self-named Wild Man bounded into the debate:

> These are countries where people starve to death. I hate these ignorant people living in the comfort of their home, just stupid and ignorant, trying to sound "moral." So do you want them to die? Do you want their families to starve and kill their babies because they don't have money for food or even proper shelter? Are you taking out your wallet to help them? You sure haven't helped them. So stop whining. If you say, here I donate $100 million dollars to help with the poverty, then I give you some credit. But all you do is talk. Don't do shit but

talk. Talk to make yourself feel superior, superior that you are not in a third world country. What if you are one of them?

This is distorted logic at its worst. If these men truly wanted to help a destitute woman, they would give her a hand up without demanding sex in return. Playing the charity card is the absolute height of hypocrisy. The actions of these global sex prowlers are directly responsible for the explosion in the trafficking of women and girls. Their insatiable demands have led to the kidnapping, forcible confinement and repeated rapes of millions of young women. And they cannot absolve themselves by saying they didn't know. Not bothering to investigate whether the women they're using have been forced into the flesh trade is akin to a murderous soldier saying "I was only following orders." And if they prowl the internet in search of sexual gratification, chances are they'll eventually trip onto a message posted by someone with a conscience, like Arab Man Observing. Then they will have no excuse.

5

DARING
SOULS

So often cars would slow down and people would yell,
"You are a whore. This is no job for a girl like you."
But they never stopped to ask if they could help me.
—STEFA, A MOLDOVAN TEENAGER TRAFFICKED INTO ITALY

FOR TRAFFICKED WOMEN and girls, there are few roads to freedom. There is rescue and there is escape. The first requires luck— whether in the form of a caring john willing to stick his neck out or as the result of a police raid. The second road—escape— demands incredible daring and courage. In one such case, a Ukrainian girl held in a brothel in Bosnia heard the rumble of heavy trucks from her second-floor prison. Looking out the window, she saw the Russian flag and the UN insignia. She jumped from the balcony and, dressed only in her underwear,

ran screaming toward the military convoy. An armored personnel carrier stopped. The heavily armed peacekeepers weren't
about to be intimidated by the thuggish bar owner. They immediately gave the girl some clothing, placed her in a jeep and later
helped her return to Ukraine.

Luck or rescue, however, is not the common path to
freedom for most trafficked women. Tragically, for them release
comes as the result of disease, insanity or total depletion. In the
end, some give up and kill themselves.

When Canadian police officer Gordon Moon signed on in
June 2000 to work for the United Nations as an international
cop in the renegade Serbian province of Kosovo, he had no idea
what he was in for. The strapping, forty-year-old Ontario
Provincial Police detective had enlisted for a stint with the UN
to help restore law and order in this tiny war-ravaged Balkan
region. He had barely gotten over his jet lag when he found
himself investigating serious crimes—murders, vicious assaults,
grenade attacks and bombings. Criminals had infiltrated every
aspect of life, and Moon realized that law enforcers faced a long
and difficult struggle to gain the upper hand.

While posted in Pristina, he noticed a disturbing trend—
young women, mostly from Moldova, Romania and Ukraine,
were showing up at the station complaining they had been
kidnapped and forced into prostitution. It didn't take long
for Moon to figure out that this was more than just a random
occurrence. But what troubled him even more was the age
and condition of these women. He decided to do something
about it.

I just felt a real passion to see that this problem was at least addressed because it hadn't been. So I went to my boss and said, "We have a serious problem here and it's not being addressed." And he said, "Well, yeah, but I don't have the men to put onto it." Anyway, I ended up talking him into giving me the time to at least investigate the matter in the Pristina area. I probably spent three-quarters of my time doing intelligence gathering and investigative work on the bars in the city and the surrounding area. The situation was really bad.

About that time a spate of bad press erupted. The local news media accused the UN command of crass indifference toward hundreds of young Slavic women being raped daily in bars and brothels across the province. In response, the UN commander called Moon and gave him the green light to move in and hit hard. The officer formed the Trafficking and Prostitution Investigation Unit and went straight to work. Backed by peacekeeping troops, his small unit began kicking down doors and raiding flesh pits.

"I would say well over 95 percent of the women and girls we pulled out of those places were trafficked," Moon recounted. "Only a very small percentage were there of their own free will."

For Moon, the level of inhumanity these women were forced to endure while in captivity was difficult to fathom. The married father of three had seen his share of crime working in the OPP photographic and video surveillance unit back home, but this was the stuff of nightmares. His unit found teenage girls chained in mud cellars. Many bore the telltale signs of torture—cigarette burn marks on their arms, welts on their backsides and bruises covering their bodies.

"The living conditions of the girls, in the majority of the cases, were appalling," Moon said, his voice rising in anger. "The girls were locked in cell-like rooms. They weren't properly fed. They didn't have clean clothes. They didn't have shower facilities. Their hygiene was disgusting. It's hard to imagine how they survived."

> We did one raid where we went to the basement and we found six girls locked up and their guard out front. Their guard would just go in as the girls were required and bring them up to a room to provide the service, and then the girls would be escorted back down and locked up again. There was no toilet so these girls were peeing in the corner of the basement. The guard would throw some food under the door, like a hamburger, in the middle of the day. That was it. Then the girls were expected to service clients from 4 p.m. right through till about three or four in the morning, and they had to perform sex acts for these guys fifteen times a night.

Moon remembered one nineteen-year-old Ukrainian university student he'd rescued from servitude. She had answered a newspaper ad to be a nanny in Italy.

> She was not a dumb girl. She just wanted to make some money so she could continue her education. The next thing you know, she's in some basement in a Belgrade house being mauled and looked over by a bunch of guys who want to buy

her. And then from there, it goes from bad to worse. Well, she ends up in Kosovo and for days she's doing sex twenty-four hours a day. Finally, we just happened to raid the place where she was being held and so we were able to rescue her.

At first, Moon thought he was making a difference. But then the disturbing reality set in. As fast as his unit pulled the girls out, they were replaced.

We raided this one bar. There were twelve girls and we took them all away. They were all trafficked and they all wanted to go home. Then two nights later, the guy who owned the bar was back in business. He just picked up the phone and called his supplier in Belgrade and ordered in another shipment. That's how easy it was. It was just a phone call. "I've been hit by the police. Let's go. We need new girls right away."

What stunned him most was how two groups, who only months earlier had been killing each other, were now setting aside centuries-old differences to capitalize on these women and make a quick buck. "What it all boiled down to was that the Serbs and the Albanians, who hate each other and are sworn mortal enemies, were able to communicate and get along when it came to organized crime and trafficking women," he said.

Moon left Kosovo in the spring of 2001, satisfied that he had done important, groundbreaking work. Still, he understood that much more had to be done to put a significant dent in the teeming flesh trade in that pathetic corner of the world.

In just six short months, the unassuming detective from the small Ontario town of Orillia had raided fifty bars and brothels in Kosovo and, together with his squad, rescued almost 300 young women. Sadly, his effort often felt more like tossing a tiny life preserver into a sea of drowning women. But Moon has a lot to be proud of. He saw a problem that had been shamefully ignored and tackled it with unrelenting determination. He made a difference.

ALTHOUGH RARE, there have been times when cries for help from far-flung places have paid off in dramatic rescues. Workers at La Strada—the nongovernmental organization dedicated to fighting the trafficking of women in Kyiv, Ukraine—received a frantic phone call in early 2000 from a mother whose daughter and several friends had been forced into prostitution in the Serbian province of Montenegro. In this instance, enough information came to light to launch an all-out emergency rescue.

Inna Shvab, a manager at La Strada, recounted that a Serb and his Ukrainian wife living in Montenegro had invited a group of eight Ukrainian women to work as waitresses at their restaurant in Podgorica. The women, ranging in age from nineteen to twenty-two, arrived in October 1999, but instead of tending tables, seven of them were sold to a nightclub owner—a former employee of the local police and a notorious thug. The eighth girl was sent to the nearby town of Budva and put to work at a dive called the Black Mont.

During the day, the bar owner kept his girls under lock and key in a cold, damp cellar. They were fed once a day and forced to service bar patrons at night. By sheer luck, one of the clients happened to have a cell phone, and one of the braver girls managed to sneak out a call to her family in the impoverished Donetsk region of eastern Ukraine. Panic-stricken, the mother turned to La Strada for help. They contacted Ann Jordan of the International Human Rights Law Group in Washington D.C., another NGO. Jordan, in turn, called U.S. Congressman Christopher H. Smith, who was then chairman of the Commission on Security and Cooperation in Europe (the Helsinki Commission). An outspoken champion of human rights, Smith was a driving force behind the U.S. government's tough anti-trafficking legislation. The politician didn't waste a second. Knowing full well that police and government corruption were rife in that part of the world, he fired off an "URGENT" fax to the prime minister of Montenegro, requesting his "immediate assistance."

Smith supplied Montenegrin authorities with all the salient details, and early the following morning a special squad of police pounced on the bars. Seven of the eight girls were rescued; the eighth had been sold to an Albanian trafficker the day before. Police also recovered a Romanian woman and two Moldovan girls. They were all transported to Belgrade and a few days later returned home. Incredibly, one of the Ukrainian women identified several of the police officers who carried out the raid as her former clients. It's not surprising that in such situations, trafficked women are reluctant to seek protection from local authorities or police.

The rescue operation was hailed as a success, but the disappearance of the eighth woman deeply upset her friends.

The authorities had no idea where she was being held. Four months later she suddenly returned home. She had been smuggled from Albania into Italy by speedboat over the Adriatic Sea and forced to work as a prostitute on a highway outside Rome. Her pimp let her go because she'd become pregnant and was of little use to him. The woman, severely scarred by the ordeal, went back to her hometown. She could not bring herself to have an abortion and decided to have the baby.

HIGH WALLS AND CHAIN-LINK FENCES surround a sprawling compound on the Adriatic coast near San Foca in the stiletto heel of southern Italy. The place is like a fortress. Video cameras scan the grounds. Armed guards patrol the perimeter and a determined security force mans the electronic gate. No one is allowed in without a nod from the person in charge—Don Cesare Lo Deserto. On any given day, this bear of a man with a round, bald head and thick farmer's hands can be spotted strolling about the property talking urgently into a cell phone. Dressed in a drab gray suit and black shirt, he has the slow, deliberate stride of a nightclub bouncer. He wears aviator-style glasses and possesses an intense stare that can at times be unnerving.

The heavy security is in place because Don Cesare has had his life threatened several times. A lot of Albanian gangsters want to see him dead or, at least, permanently out of their way. Don Cesare has upset their criminal order by taking "goods" they believe don't belong to him, and on a few occasions they have attempted to take their property back. The don, however, is not afraid, and has no intention of giving in to their demands. Safely ensconced in a half-dozen bungalow-style units at the north end of the compound are ninety young women from Eastern Europe, mostly from Moldova, Romania and Ukraine. All had been smuggled into Italy by Albanian pimps to work the streets. That is, until Don Cesare found them and shepherded them to his compound. Throughout the region, the women are known as Don Cesare's girls, and the place they now call home is Regina Pacis.

It is a safe house. Don Cesare is a Roman Catholic priest, and his mission in life is to rescue women from the seedy streets of Italian cities. It is a calling that, more than once, has brought him in close range of losing his life. Albanian mobsters don't take kindly to holy people relieving them of their livelihood. On one occasion, early in February 2001, two thugs showed up to persuade the priest to butt out of their affairs. Don Cesare was out on an evening stroll along the beach across from his compound when the two Albanian men emerged from the nearby woods.

> When they approached, they acted with a great deal of respect. They did not wear masks and one of them spoke fluent Italian. Then I saw the pistol. They told me very calmly to walk with them. We went to a wooded area not too far away. They were totally relaxed about it. Once we reached the woods, they began to threaten me. They told me they bought these women, that they were their property and they were demanding that I restore their property. They

also warned me of the consequences my rescues might have—both for me and for the girls.

Their message was clear.

Concerned about the length of time the priest had been gone, a team of Carabinieri officers from the center set out to look for him. As the officers came near, the culprits made a run for it.

Recounting it months later in his sparse office at the center, Don Cesare doesn't seem the least bit flustered. The way he sees it, he is doing God's work, and who better to have on your side for protection? Today, however, whenever he ventures outside the compound three armed bodyguards are never far from his side.

Just fifty meters from the center, the azure waters of the Adriatic cascade rhythmically onto the shore. Don Cesare gazes out into the distance, wondering what the sea will bring in the coming nights. Just beyond the horizon, across the narrow Straits of Otranto, only forty-four nautical miles separate Italy from Albania. On the other side lies Vlorë—the staging dock for a modern slave trade that crisscrosses Europe. Every night, under the cloak of darkness, with the Cape of Otranto light-house as a guide, Albanian smugglers leave the town on their *scafi*—motorized rubber dinghies. They race across the strait, hoping to elude the Italian coast guard. Italy's long and winding coast is almost impossible to patrol. In fact, the government has called for greater international coordination to combat the smuggling and what it has described as "one of the most dangerous organized crime networks operating in the Mediterranean."

For the past decade, Albanian smugglers have continued to outrun the Italian coast guard. When they're being hotly pursued, the *scafisti* resort to unimaginable maneuvers. To evade capture, they toss their human cargo overboard. With the coast guard scrambling to rescue the women from the choppy waters, the smugglers retreat to the relative safety of the Albanian coast. Even more tragic, numerous boats have capsized in sudden storms, leaving victims' bodies washing up on shore.

Shaking his head in disgust, the forty-two-year-old priest finds it difficult to understand the depth of cruelty to which men will sink in order to make money off another human being. Don Cesare is not a preachy man. A tiny cross dangling below his white collar is the only sign of his vocation. The veteran of missions to Brazil, Rwanda and Madagascar is low-key. He never pushes religion on the rescued women.

In the mid-1990s, returning to his native Puglia province, he witnessed the boats of misery disgorging their human cargo daily off the shores of Italy—a flood of refugees fleeing war-ravaged Yugoslavia and countries beyond. In 1995 he founded Regina Pacis in a former children's summer camp compound and flung the doors wide open to the poor and destitute.

Four years later tens of thousands of UN peacekeepers arrived in Kosovo and Bosnia-Herzegovina and the mass exodus abated. The priest, however, began to notice a disturbing change in the human cargo smuggled onto Italian beaches—thousands of young, attractive women from Moldova, Romania, Russia and Ukraine. He was shocked when he learned their true fate, and decided, then and there, that he wanted to help. Walling off an annex of the compound, he set out to give these young women another chance. By his own count, Don Cesare has saved more than 1000 women from the clutches of Albanian flesh dealers over the last ten years. Most had crossed the Adriatic after a forced trek through the Balkans, having survived Serbian breaking grounds before the final dash to the West. By the time they reach the boats, they are no longer girls. They have been hardened for the streets.

When you meet them, now safe, at Regina Pacis, most look like fragile, frightened children. For them, happiness is a faded memory. Their innocence is shattered, their pale, gaunt faces etched with the lines of incredible suffering and humiliation. Yet when they see Don Cesare, they always manage a smile. To them, he is their savior. To the priest, they are heroines. They are the ones who reached deep inside and found the courage to run, to escape from their captors. They are the ones who survived a hellish journey and are now trying to rebuild their lives. The priest has a fondness for a special group: those who have had the courage to give birth to babies conceived in prostitution and rape. More than three dozen children have been born at Regina Pacis. Several boys have been christened Cesare, and one Moldovan girl is called Cesaria.

Don Cesare has heard the laments of each and every woman who has come through the gates to Regina Pacis. He knows and understands their reality and dismisses any suggestion that some may have chosen to walk the streets. "Most of them leave home without knowing," he said. "It is true that some know, but knowing does not mean wanting."

DON CESARE INVITES ME for a stroll through the compound. As we enter the area where the women live, the priest is greeted with warmth and adoration. Every woman receives a kind word and a sympathetic ear. He doesn't rush and his patience seems endless.

One woman stands by a doorway sobbing into her kerchief. The priest approaches slowly and asks what is wrong. She says she misses home but is too ashamed to go back, convinced that her family and friends will shun her and call her a whore. Taking her hand, Don Cesare tells her she needs time to heal and, until she's ready to return home, her home is here.

Every woman at Regina Pacis has survived a hundred nightmares. They walk close together, clinging to each other for support. They talk in furtive whispers. They jump at sudden noises and stare at strangers with dread. Most times, though, they simply sit in silence, lost in their thoughts.

Don Cesare introduces me to Irina, a twenty-year-old raven-haired Romanian. She has been at the center for almost a year and will be returning to her family in Bucharest soon. She speaks fluent Italian, Moldovan and Ukrainian. Her hair is shoulder-length and her complexion ashen. Her green eyes emit no emotion. Her expression is hard and untrusting. Yet, she is polite and helpful, asking that I wait outside the bungalow that houses five other women while they put on a fresh pot of coffee.

Sitting at the table with two other women—Stefa, a black-haired seventeen-year-old Moldovan, and Lesia, a striking nineteen-year-old Ukrainian—Irina pours everyone a cup of coffee. Lesia starts telling her story but is quickly overwhelmed with emotion. She grabs a cigarette and shakes her head frantically, saying she can no longer continue. Irina now turns to Stefa.

Holding her hand, Irina asks her what had happened to her. Stefa takes a sip of coffee and stares down at the table. There is a deep sadness in her eyes and a quaver in her voice. She too is clearly uncomfortable and the memories, although still fresh, are difficult to summon on command. In a barely audible whisper, she begins her tale.

Stefa's horror began eight months earlier in Chisinau, the capital of Moldova, the poorest country in Europe. She was just sixteen, straight out of high school. All she wanted was a job as a waitress or maid so that she could help out her family.

"I was with my girlfriend Katrina. We went to Romania with her boyfriend to look for work. He told us he knew a man that could give us a job cleaning rooms in a hotel."

Instead, the girls were sold to a trafficker.

We were taken to an apartment building near Belgrade. There were many, many girls, perhaps as many as sixty, from Ukraine, Russia, Romania, Moldova and Bulgaria.

I cannot describe the horror that went on there. A few times a day, the owner would come and yell at us to get ready, buyers were coming. At all hours these men arrived and we would have to take off our clothes and stand in front of them. They wanted to see what we looked like naked. They touched us and examined us like we were cattle. Sometimes they took us to a room to see how we performed sexually.

Stefa's eyes began to well up with tears.

My friend Katrina was purchased after two weeks. I cried so much when they took her away. All I can remember was the terrified look in her eyes and the tears rolling down her face. She was shaking so terribly. I remained in the apartment for three more weeks before I was bought. In that time, so many more new girls arrived to replenish those who had been sold.

I don't know what price I was sold for. An Albanian man named Geko bought me and another girl from Ukraine and smuggled us by rubber boat into Italy. On the ride over, the weather was terrible. It was raining and the waves were high. I held on to the sides, thinking we would overturn and I would drown. When we arrived on shore, a car met us and we were taken to Mestra, outside Venice. We were taken to a small apartment. Four girls lived there. Geko told me to take a shower and when I came out, he threw me on the bed and raped me.

Stefa's hands begin to shake uncontrollably as she describes him. "He was a short, hideous man with a red face, rotten teeth and terrible breath." She pauses for a sip of coffee and a long, hard drag on a cigarette. The room is deathly quiet. The women sharing the quarters weep in silence, reliving their own private hell in their thoughts.

When the pimp was finished, he tossed her a sheet of paper bearing words and phrases in Italian for sexual acts she was required to perform and the price for each act. He instructed her to memorize them. He also told her she was to be on the street at seven every night of the week whether it was raining, snowing or sweltering, and she could not leave until she had earned him $500 a night.

> I had to wear a mini-skirt, a thin blouse with nothing under-neath and this ugly makeup. So often cars would slow down and people would yell, "You are a whore. This is no job for a girl like you." But they never stopped to ask if they could help me. They simply drove away, so smug and judging. They didn't know my circumstances. In their eyes I was a whore. They believed I *wanted* to be on that street selling my body and, as such, deserved my fate. It was so far from the truth.

Stefa suddenly stops and gets up from the table. She apologizes and lights up another cigarette. She needs a moment to recover. Four of her roommates gather around her and they all hug. She returns and pours herself another espresso, sits down at the table and resumes her story.

"I wanted to escape but I was scared. Geko was very mean and told me he would find me and kill me if I tried to leave. I had no one to turn to. I didn't know where to go. I didn't know the language. My life had become this black existence."

Every day was a bad day for Stefa, but sometimes there were really bad days.

> My worst was when two men picked me up and we went to a nearby parking lot. One of them grabbed me by the throat. I thought he was going to kill me. I pleaded with them not to kill me. They robbed me and forced me to have sex with them. When they were finished, they threw me onto the roadside like a piece of garbage and drove away. As they left, one of them yelled from the window, "Say hello to Geko."

Every single night Stefa cried while standing on street corners, praying that she'd be rescued, but it wasn't to be. "Once a man saw me crying and told me to go to the police. He thought it was so easy, this solution. I was afraid of the police. I was afraid of everything. Geko told all the girls the police would do terrible things to us in the jail if we were arrested. He said they were corrupt. That he had paid them off. So every time I saw them, I ran away."

Then one day, Stefa felt she could no longer take it. She decided anything was better than this life, even prison. She mustered what little courage she had and went to the local police station. Standing in front of a long, wooden counter, she could sense the indifference and condescension in the police officer's eyes.

"I was told by this officer that he couldn't help me. He said, 'You can't come here and tell us this.' I didn't know where to go, where to turn, what to do and I started to cry. The policeman then told me to go to Milan where there was the Moldova consulate. I left the police station. I had no money so I hitch-hiked to Milan."

When Stefa finally arrived at the consulate, the resident counselor was indifferent to her plight and curtly told her there was no money in the budget to send her back home. Stefa broke down. The bureaucrat nervously riffled through his in-basket, picked up the phone and placed a call to Regina Pacis. A few hours later Stefa was on a bus bound for Lecce. She had finally escaped.

"I was on the street for four months in all," she said. In that brief period, she was used by hundreds of men and figures that Geko made at least $60,000 off her body.

When Stefa settled into Regina Pacis, her greatest fear wasn't getting tracked down by her pimp. It was calling home.

My parents did not know what had happened to me. I told my mother and she said she knew. She had gone to a card reader and was told. She prayed I would be rescued and her prayers were answered. All she wants is that I return home. I don't know when that will be. All I know is I want to stay here for a while and collect my thoughts. I want to be alone. I need peace of mind. I need to feel safe and secure. Don Cesare says he will help me find a job in a hotel in the summer so I can make a little money before I finally go home.

Something else continues to trouble Stefa.

Many times, I've thought about Katrina. When I arrived at Regina Pacis, I called her home. Her parents were frantic.

They hadn't heard a word from her since she left. They asked me if I knew anything. I froze. I did not know what to say. So I pretended the line went dead. I was afraid to tell her parents what had happened to their daughter.

At night, when I go to bed, I pray. I pray my parents believe me that I was forced, that I am not a bad girl, that I am not a prostitute. I am afraid to close my eyes to sleep because when I do, all I see is pain. I see the faces of all those men and I see Geko. I just want to forget . . . but I can't.

Stefa gets up from the table, tears rolling down her cheeks. She goes into her room and falls onto her bed and sobs.

ON A STARLIT EVENING, as the smugglers in Vlorë are readying their speedboats on the Albanian side of the Adriatic, Don Cesare flings open the gates of Regina Pacis and leads a small procession of women across the narrow road to the edge of the rocky beach. They stand, silently facing the sea they had crossed. The priest raises his arms, blesses the rolling waves and begins to pray. The women stare out onto the water, their lips moving in prayer for the victims who have yet to be rescued.

A couple of nights later, as I was driving along Via Solaria outside Rome, the "nighttime butterflies," as they are called in Italy, were out in full force. On the edge of the bustling thoroughfare, in the dark side roads, their pimps sat watching their property in secondhand cars through tinted windows. For these young women, escape will not come easily.

6

A MATTER OF
INDIFFERENCE

*The vice trade is one which people can, if they wish to,
turn a blind eye to, but I fail to see how we as
a mature society can turn our backs on people.*
—CHIEF SUPERINTENDENT SIMON HUMPHREY
OF SCOTLAND YARD

IN A TYPICAL BROTHEL RAID or street sweep in cosmopolitan cities throughout the world, foreign prostitutes are rounded up and charged. For the most part, the authorities don't treat these women as victims of crime; they are regarded simply as illegal migrants. No attempt is made to determine whether they were trafficked. They are jailed, processed for immigration or labor violations and deported as quickly as possible. Innocent women, in other words, are stigmatized and then victimized over and over again.

Evidence of government complacency is staggering. International studies and reports are replete with examples of blatant and overwhelming insensitivity. Yet despite the damning reports detailing what's been occurring openly throughout the Western world year after year, and despite the tragic testimonials of thousands of victims, the prevailing attitude among the very people who should know better crosses into the realm of criminal neglect.

Once in the clutches of traffickers and pimps, women get little sympathy from government officials or the public in general. Most times, they are met with apathy and scorn. After all, they've been working the streets. And it is there on the streets that they first slam up against the biggest hurdle of indifference—the police. They learn quickly that the man on the beat cares little about them and that there is absolutely no upside in running to him for protection. It is a complacency that plays directly into the hands of organized crime and makes it that much easier for low-life criminals to get into the trade.

Comments from officials like Gennadi Lepenko, chief of Interpol in Kyiv, Ukraine—"Women's groups want to blow this all out of proportion"—serve only to exacerbate the situation. So do explanations such as the one offered to monitors with the International Helsinki Federation for Human Rights in June 2000. According to K. Goryainov, a high-ranking bureaucrat with the Russian Ministry of the Interior,

> This problem does not really bother the Ministry of the Interior. There is no criminality in it. All the violations of law

committed against these women take place already in the territories of the countries that they leave for. Hence, it's those countries' problem. All in all, the polemic about trafficking in women has come to us from the West. All the noise made on the subject is bolstered by the adventurist feminist organizations that promise to help but in reality render no assistance to the victims. They receive grants and for financial compensation spread information that has nothing to do with reality.

It is precisely this kind of thinking that fosters apathy toward trafficking victims. And even in nations that talk the talk, pockets of indifference abound.

In Sweden, where the government has led a vociferous attack on traffickers, police in the northernmost province of Norrbotten were soundly criticized by the nation's Central Police Command in February 2003 for laziness in their investigations of the sex trade. The Norrbotten police had information on dozens of Russian women believed to be imported into the province to work as prostitutes, the names of several men suspected of trafficking them to Sweden and numerous reported suspicions of trafficking in the area. And yet in the preceding year only one preliminary investigation had been launched.

Human Rights Watch uncovered a particularly disturbing example of benign indifference during a 2001 investigation of the trafficking trade in Greece. They learned that Romanian police had received a frantic call from a terrified mother in October 2000. Her daughter had just phoned pleading to be rescued from the Tutti Frutti bar on the Greek island of Kos where she was being held as a sex slave. The police immediately contacted the International Organization for Migration office in Bucharest. IOM staff fired off an urgent fax to Daniel Esdras, their counterpart in Athens. This communication was no vague missive—it listed the name of the island, the town, the bar where the young woman was being held, the trafficker's name, his home and cell phone numbers, as well as the victim's name, description and place of residence in Romania. The fax also included the name and numbers of a top official with the Greek Ministry of Public Order who had represented Greece at a recent UN-sponsored conference on trafficking human beings. With a contact like that, action was certain.

Esdras relayed the fax—entitled "Police Action to Rescue a Romanian Victim of Trafficking"—to the official. He also pleaded with Greek authorities not to deport the woman. "I told them the IOM would handle and pay for her repatriation," Esdras said. Then he waited . . . and never received a reply.

A month later, during the Human Rights Watch fact-finding mission, Esdras recounted the incident of the Romanian woman. HRW investigators placed a call to the ministry to find out what had happened with the case and were shocked at what they learned. Little had been done. The police paid what amounted to a courtesy visit to the alleged trafficker, who said he had sent the woman back to Romania. The cops accepted the bar owner's statement and left. That was the extent of the entire investigation.

So whatever happened to the young Romanian woman? Did she end up returning home? In response to an email sent

April 18, 2002, Cristian Ionescu, an information officer at the
IOM Bucharest office, wrote: "I regret to inform you that we
have not been able to track this victim of human trafficking
since then." As this case so tragically illustrates, trafficked
women cannot rely on Greek authorities for effective protection
or for assistance with safe repatriation to their homeland.

Even where good laws exist, people trafficking is considered
a far less serious crime than smuggling guns or drugs and so
remains a low enforcement priority in most sending and destination countries. Officials in the receiving nations are quick to
blame former Soviet states and East Bloc countries like Russia,
Ukraine, Moldova, Romania and Bulgaria for allowing its most
vulnerable women and girls to be trafficked virtually at will.
Still, the hard reality is that most of the victims of trafficking
end up in brothels in the European Union, North America, the
Middle East and the Far East. It is the demand for cheap and
available sex that has ignited the trafficking explosion in the
receiving countries, and these nations are doing very little to
stop it.

The complacency begins in gleaming government office
towers and trickles all the way down to the gutters. If the
political masters and senior bureaucrats don't view the trafficking
in women and girls as serious, that attitude will eventually
infect every level of the legal system—from the courts to the
cop on the beat. And this is precisely what has been happening worldwide.

In a high-profile trial that took place in Linz, Austria, in
October 2001, Hellmuth Suessenbacher, known as the

Carinthian Porno King, was convicted of trafficking fifty Romanian women into the local sex trade. They were initially hired as dancers and then forced into prostitution. To gasps of disbelief, Suessenbacher was sentenced to a mere two and a half years in prison. The convicted gangster appealed his sentence, and a year later Austria's Court of Appeal reduced it to two years.

Indifference toward trafficked women appears to be par for the course in the office of Israel's attorney general. It has issued guidelines to the police not to hassle brothels unless a woman complains that she's being kept there against her will or a member of the public complains that the brothel is causing a disturbance. Ironically, these guidelines fly in the face of Israeli law. Although prostitution is not illegal, operating a brothel and pimping are.

Nomi Levenkron, an outspoken Israeli human rights lawyer, argues that the guidelines "bluntly ignore the reality known to all parties involved: that most of the women working in brothels are in fact kept there against their will and they are unable to file a complaint in the police station."

In an interview at her tiny office at the Hotline for Migrant Workers in Tel Aviv, Levenkron charged that "the attitude of Israeli society in general and Israeli authorities in particular to the issue of trafficking in women is tainted by indifference, prejudice and ignorance. All these arise from the fact that even today we live in a predominantly male society, which is preoccupied with burning security issues and not humanitarian ones."

Since the victims of trafficking are

female, foreign and prostitutes, committing a crime against such a victim is not viewed as severe enough. This means that the police are not inclined to investigate crimes against prostitutes, and that the attorney general is not eager to add these issues to their already overinflated caseloads. This attitude of the Israeli authorities makes trafficking a profitable and risk-free business. It is no wonder, then, that this industry is rapidly growing.

One of the main culprits behind this growth is the judiciary, Levenkron continued. "Due to great workloads and often total ignorance and indifference, the courts dismiss the pimps and the traffickers with light punishments."

Human rights advocates point out that while the maximum punishment for trading in human beings in Israel is sixteen years, sentencing overall amounts to a joke. Cases are routinely disposed of through plea bargains. Some of the decisions are unfathomable and an insult to the dignity and suffering of trafficked women. In March 2002, for example, an Israeli policeman was convicted of buying a trafficked woman and of warning brothel owners about impending police raids. His sentence: six months' community service. Although the judge noted that the plea bargain was "exceptionally lenient" considering the matter involved a corrupt cop, he nonetheless accepted the plea without challenge.

In another plea bargain involving two pimps, Judge Natan Amit leveled a sharp rebuke at Israeli authorities:

This is a picture of the Ugly Israel that the law enforcement authorities are not capable of changing. A young girl, who has just reached maturity, is brought here illegally from her homeland. On arrival, she receives a forged identity and immediately becomes a sex slave in a massage parlor, as these places are called. When the law enforcers are asked why they do not act against so-called escort services that are illegal, they reply that the policy is to ignore them unless they disturb the neighbors.

Yet Judge Amit also accepted the plea bargain, sentencing one pimp to community service and the other to three years.

For prosecutors, plea bargains are all about saving money on lengthy, expensive trials. It doesn't matter if it results in a mere slap on the wrist; they earn a conviction and it appears as if something has been done. In the process, the women—the victims—are overlooked, and by not getting their day in court, they are victimized once again. Police and prosecutors argue that plea bargains are a necessary evil because trafficking cases are often weak and chances of a conviction are almost nil. They maintain that the women steadfastly refuse to come forward to testify, making it virtually impossible to build a criminal case against the pimps, brothel owners and traffickers.

When I asked Levenkron about this, she countered that it is simply not true. She has come across many cases where "the women are not informed by the police of their right to testify against their offenders. Furthermore, it is not difficult to under-stand the fear of these women." They are very much aware of the fate that awaits them after the trial—"deportation to their home countries, where the contact men who had sent them in the first place wait 'with open arms.' It is easy to understand the fear of those unwilling to testify, while the ones willing to testify find themselves facing cops who are not willing to investigate."

This is the dire reality that trafficked women face, not only in Israel but in most countries. They're told by police and prosecutors that criminal charges will be laid against their tormentors but only if they agree to testify against them. These are women who have been brutalized and terrorized by their pimps. They are afraid for their very lives. Yet in the vast majority of cases they're not offered witness protection. It's no wonder that most choose deportation instead. Those who do summon the courage to testify live in constant fear of retribution once they're deported, and with good reason. Many women who have testified have been killed upon their return. Levenkron knows of two cases in which women were murdered shortly after they testified against their pimps in 1995. "I haven't seen the documents. I only heard it from the police. They told me two women were sent back home. A few days later a telegram came from the Russian embassy saying that both were killed."

Amnesty International documented yet another case in which a woman who testified against her traffickers disappeared after being deported. The woman, named Tatiana, had arrived in Israel from Belarus in April 1998 on a tourist visa. She had been promised a job as a cleaner in the seaside resort of Eilat. All she wanted was a job that would pay her enough to support her mother and her six-year-old son back home. When she landed, a man pretending to be from the hotel met her at the airport. He drove her to a brothel where she was locked up and put to work against her will. Tatiana tried to escape on several occasions but was caught each time.

Her freedom came several months later in a police raid on the brothel. She was taken into custody as an illegal immigrant and detained in Neveh Tirza prison to await deportation. Three days after her arrest she found an anonymous note on her prison bunk. The author threatened to kill her and punish her family if she spoke out about her case. Tatiana was adamant about testifying against her captors, but was also terrified that if she did so they would track her down when she returned home. Her lawyers filed an urgent petition with the Israeli authorities explaining that if Tatiana was not given witness protection, it would be unreasonably dangerous for her to testify in court. The terse reply: Israeli police could not guarantee anyone's safety outside the country.

Tatiana decided to testify nonetheless and in June 1999 she was deported. Before she was taken to the airport she made one final plea—that she be flown to Poland or Lithuania and allowed to cross into Belarus by car. Her request was denied, and she was shipped directly to Belarus. At the airport in Minsk she was reportedly met by a man who briskly escorted her to a waiting car. Tatiana's fate after that is unknown.

WHILE IT'S DIFFICULT to comprehend the wall of complacency trafficked women face each and every day, there is an ugly reality behind it—racism. Most human rights activists working to stop the traffic don't like to admit this publicly. It's one of those hot-button subjects that percolates very near the surface but is best left for discussion behind closed doors. It's a racism based in a community's deep-seated fear that their men are out on the prowl and that innocent local girls will be sexually assaulted and raped. The cold translation: better them than ours.

In a comfortable apartment in a Tel Aviv suburb, Leah Gruenpeter-Gold and Nissan Ben-Ami, co-directors of the Awareness Center—the nongovernmental group that specializes in research on trafficking in women and prostitution in Israel— recall the day in June 2001 when "the pimps came to the Knesset." The pimps had gathered to testify before a parliamentary committee looking into the trafficking issue in Israel. The opinions put forth would, at times, venture into the realm of the absurd.

Ben-Ami spoke of an Arab-Israeli lawyer who argued for the necessity of brothels:

> He said it is better to open legal brothels in East Jerusalem than continue to handle the harsh phenomenon of sexual crimes in the family there, which is due to the fact that there are many satellite dishes on the roofs with all sorts of porno films that are arousing the appetite of men.
>
> What the lawyer said is, because of the sexual frustration of Palestinian men, we need to organize trafficking of women to Israel and to the Palestinian Authority or else they will rape our daughters. In order to protect Arab girls from rape, he proposed the trafficking of women from Russia.

Gruenpeter-Gold described the testimony of a man she referred to as the "lawyer to the pimps."

He told the committee sex is like food and his clients decided to raise the level of prostitution in Israel so that men will have gourmet . . . so they will have a better choice because Russian prostitutes are better than Israeli prostitutes. In other words, Israeli prostitutes are not good so we have to organize highly educated Russian prostitutes in order to satisfy the good taste of Israeli men.

The underlying message, Ben-Ami said with disgust, was clear: "You don't want girls from your family or your own neighborhood to be prostitutes. You want girls from abroad."

Yossi Sedbon, police commander of the Tel Aviv district, stunned participants at a conference on prostitution and trafficking at Beit Berl College in February 2001. He began by complaining that anyone "who thinks this phenomenon can be eliminated doesn't know what he is talking about" and maintained that his officers were doing their best to combat the burgeoning sex trade. His tone, however, exuded not determination but resignation. He went on to blame those who he felt were directly responsible for creating the crisis: "There are now about 200,000 foreign workers and tens of thousands of Palestinians living in the Tel Aviv area. What can you do? They simply need sex services."

Levenkron shook her head in disbelief.

What he is saying is the presence of foreign prostitutes serves as a vent for the sexual needs of the migrant community, thus keeping them from raping innocent Israeli women. How easy it is to blame "them" for the ills of the Israeli

society. This claim borders on the ridiculous, since the prostitutes themselves claim that the majority of their clients are
Israeli. The fact is the biggest users are Israeli men, then Arab
men and then migrant workers. When we talk to the women
about their clients, they say, "Do you think migrant workers
have enough money for this?"

In the north part of Tel Aviv, the biggest group of Israelis
frequenting the brothels—and the women know how to recognize them—are the religious men. They are about one-third of
their clients. Women show us how they take off their *kippa*
[skull cap] and push their *payes* [sidelocks] behind their ears.

The fact that racism—better them than our girls—is a
reality in so many countries explains the rampant indifference
toward trafficked women from all levels of government.

In an interview with the BBC's current affairs TV show
Assignment on August 17, 2002, Chief Superintendent Simon
Humphrey of Scotland Yard, head of the London vice squad,
suggested that trafficking in women hasn't been a priority
because the victims aren't British:

> I'm sure that that suggestion would be refuted, but I cannot
> understand why it is not being treated more seriously at a
> political level at the moment. Just because the majority of the
> women in this industry are from Eastern Europe, it should
> not be a reason for not treating it with the utmost serious-
> ness, because we're dealing with crimes against humanity.
> The vice trade is one which people can, if they wish to, turn
> a blind eye to, but I fail to see how we as a mature society can
> turn our backs on people.

Tinges of racism were evident in a formal presentation to South Korean government bureaucrats in 1996. An earnest Kim Kyoung Sa, president of the Korean Special Tourism Association, exhorted the committee to import "foreign entertainers" for the copious bars and strip clubs catering exclusively to U.S. soldiers from the nearby military bases in South Korea. Kim, a bar owner, lamented that Korean girls didn't want to do this kind of work anymore, which, he noted, was good thing. Economic times had vastly improved in the country and Korean girls were no longer destitute. They now had jobs in factories and office towers where they didn't have to take off their clothes to earn a living. This left the bar owners in the lurch. As a result, he explained, they needed fresh talent. To drive the point home, the club owner stressed that it was necessary to import foreign women so American soldiers would abstain from sexually harassing innocent Korean girls. As far as Kim and his cronies were concerned, his association was doing the government a big favor that would also contribute immensely to improving U.S.–Korean relations.

Sometimes racist attitudes find their way to the bench. Oleksander Mazur has seen it first-hand. In October 2001 I was sitting outside a courtroom in downtown Pristina, Kosovo, waiting for Mazur when he suddenly burst through the doors and stormed into the corridor.

The Ukrainian cop, on assignment with the United Nations as an international police officer, was absolutely livid. He'd been involved in the rescue of six young women from Moldova and Romania. The girls, barely teenagers, had been held as sex slaves in a cesspool of a brothel in nearby Ferrazaj. It had taken the policeman several days and incredible patience to convince them to testify against the brothel owners.

"I am told by the prosecutor that the judge does not want to believe the girls were forced to work as prostitutes. He thinks they are liars. He feels, Why should he take their word over the word of the bar owner? The man is corrupt. He does not want to hear the truth," Mazur said, slamming his hand against the wall.

"What are you going to do?" I asked.

"I am still trying to find out if the judge will hear the case this morning. We cannot hold these girls in Kosovo much longer. They must be sent back home, and if that happens, we have no case against the pimps."

For several minutes he rants, complaining that despite all the raids on brothels and rescues of enslaved young women, in this unruly corner of the world there are few meaningful trials and virtually no convictions.

"This is because of the level of corruption. Judges suddenly drop cases and no one knows why. But I do. What you have is an Albanian judge sitting in judgment against an Albanian man whose accuser is a Moldovan woman who doesn't speak the language."

Mazur explains that the Albanian judge is faced with a case that pits his religion, his people and his culture against a woman he thinks of as nothing more than a whore. "Also the pimp, this bar owner, is a nice guy, an upstanding person in the community. He is rich and he is helping to finance the Kosovo Liberation Army. So he is a hero. All this is connected."

IN THE NETHERWORLD of the illegal flesh trade, trafficked women repeatedly slam up against thick stone walls of complacency, racism and indifference. These are tremendous obstacles for the women to overcome. But if there is one factor that virtually seals their fate, it is corruption.

FOR A FISTFUL
OF DOLLARS

There was an actual price for touching each part of the body.
Sort of like a meat chart. The going price was $2 for the breast,
$3 for the buttock and $5 for genital contact.
—MICHAEL BAYER, SPECIAL AGENT WITH THE U.S. STATE
DEPARTMENT BUREAU OF DIPLOMATIC SECURITY

CORRUPTION IS THE GRAPNEL of the vast, brutal trade in women and girls. Trafficking thrives because of it, and could not exist to the extent that it does without it. Cash and free sex are the driving forces. As long as there are government officials with their hands out or cops with their pants down, the trade will continue to flourish.

To make money, brothel owners and pimps have to make their victims readily available to clients, night in and night out.

It is virtually impossible, therefore, to run an underground sex-trafficking enterprise. Johns have to know where to find these women whenever the urge strikes. Their quest has to be simple. They're not about to enter into a complicated game of cat and mouse and at the same time risk confrontation with the law. So it stands to reason that if lustful men can readily zero in on the traffic, the police with their investigative abilities and high-tech equipment should be able to stop the trade. Yet they don't. Why?

Gary Haugen knows the answer. As head of the International Justice Mission, a Christian-based human rights agency in Washington, D.C., he's kicked down the doors of numerous steamy Third World brothels to rescue girls from sexual slavery. Haugen's field experience has taught him one crucial lesson:

> [Traffickers, pimps and brothel keepers] are impervious to the power of the international community's resolutions, treaties, covenants and protocols—unless they impact the conduct of the police officers or constables in their streets. Unless the brothel keeper actually gets in serious trouble with the civil authorities he's going to keep doing what he's doing. There is just too much money to be made.

Martina Vandenberg, an adept, dauntless researcher who has investigated the trade for Human Rights Watch in trafficking hot spots like Bosnia, Israel and Greece, shares this view: "The human rights violation of trafficking in persons cannot flourish without the complicity of indifferent and corrupt state officials." Vandenberg has spoken to hundreds of trafficking victims and the human rights workers who work closely with them. She has heard numerous distressing stories of police and state complicity and corruption:

> Traffickers often use bribes—sometimes in the form of cash, sometimes free sexual services—to entice police and officials to look the other way, to gain protection and to circumvent supposedly impenetrable borders. Complicity not only guarantees impunity for traffickers; it sends a message to trafficked women that their traffickers enjoy impunity and that they cannot escape.

Vandenberg's sentiments were echoed in February 2002 at a trafficking conference organized by the International Helsinki Federation for Human Rights in Vienna. During two days of intense meetings, human rights activists repeatedly raised concerns about the role of state authorities in the trafficking cycle. Participants reported several examples of corruption, complicity and complacency on the part of government officials, police, border guards and court officials in many countries of origin, transit and final destination. The sordid tales also involved UN peacekeepers and the staff of numerous international aid organizations.

In one abhorrent incident cited at the Vienna conference, border guards in Poland participated in the abduction of two Ukrainian women. The guards forcibly removed the women from a bus and turned them over to traffickers in a waiting car. The women were taken to a hotel near Warsaw, where they were sold at an auction held under the protection of the local police station.

Another human rights worker at the conference recounted an informal meeting with police officials in Moldova, where corruption linked to trafficking is entrenched at the highest levels of government. The worker was warned "mildly and diplomatically" by police not to put too much hope or effort into anti-trafficking campaigns and activities. They will fail, she was told, "because important and powerful people are involved in this business."

Corruption in the trafficking trade is so well established that it can constrict the efforts of those who work with rescued women. This was made clear at a June 2002 seminar on trafficking held in Portoroz, Slovenia. At the close of the proceedings the delegates sent an urgent letter to the Council of Europe, which sponsored the event:

> In the course of the Portoroz seminar, representatives of anti-trafficking organizations declared that some of them had been under pressure by government officials not to provide information on corruption problems. Some of the NGOs were exposed to direct warnings by government representatives of the countries [they work in] before and during the conference. They have been instructed how to report on the situation considering the topics of trafficking and especially corruption. There is a notion that some of the NGOs avoided to speak openly about corruption cases facing the representatives of the governmental bodies. One would believe that the reason for such behaviour is the fear to

confront the same governmental representatives who they have to cooperate with back in their home countries on the counter trafficking activities.

In myriad reports compiled since 2000, the U.S. State Department has identified a litany of former Soviet states and East Bloc nations where corruption is a way of life. In its Country Reports on Human Rights released in March 2002, it found that in Belarus "there is existing data to the effect that corrupt militiamen are involved" in trafficking women and girls. Another on Bulgaria says, "Women do not trust the police in cases where they need to report forced prostitution and trafficking. Profits are so huge that police may be bribed." The report notes that corruption has reached "massive proportions" in that country. The same report on Georgia points out that citizens "do not trust the police because of the very high level of corruption among policemen. For example, they are aware of the districts with prostitutes and are aware of under age prostitution, but do nothing to stop these activities. They work in collaboration [with pimps] and profit themselves from the business." The Country Report on Moldova cites "widespread corruption and the connections of government officials and police with organized crime groups" in the trafficking chain.

Corruption in Russia has been cited repeatedly in numerous reports as a key factor behind the trade. They note that Russian women "cannot find the courage to approach police with complaints against the agencies that recruited them once they are back in Russia. The reason for their passivity evidently lies in the fear of organized crime and a general lack of trust in Russian law enforcement organs." The same is true in Ukraine, where "local militia and border guards received bribes in return for ignoring trafficking." Some reports allege that "local public officials abetted or assisted organized criminal groups in trafficking women abroad."

And it's not just the former Soviet states and East Bloc nations that wallow in corruption. The kind of money, power and influence that organized crime generates from the sex industry makes it easy for criminals to target greedy government officials and cops worldwide. International reports and studies are filled with such accounts wherever trafficked women end up. Without doubt the worst kind of corruption involves the police, whose job it is to serve and protect the people, and the weakest link in this chain of command is usually the cop on the beat. The violation of duties ranges from passivity— ignoring, tolerating or avoiding action—to deliberate obstruction of investigations, including warning criminals of impending raids and accepting bribes and sexual favors. And two countries that should know better from a human rights perspective and that have come under severe international criticism for police corruption in the trafficking trade are Greece and Israel.

Greece has been rocked repeatedly by allegations of rampant police corruption. For the procurers of an estimated 20,000 foreign women—mostly from Ukraine, Russia, Moldova, Bulgaria, Romania and Albania—paying for police protection is a normal business transaction. The women are smuggled in right under the watchful eyes of Greek border

guards and police to work as unregistered prostitutes in brothels, bars and massage parlors. The result: Greece has become a
magnet for sex tourism. Before the fall of the Iron Curtain, it
had no more than 2000 so-called illegal prostitutes, mostly
locals. Today, the visibility of the street trade is truly staggering.

Gregoris Lazos, a professor at Athens' Pantheon University
who headed a decade-long study of prostitution trends,
concluded that Greece has become a major global "processing
center" for East European prostitutes. He found that many of
the women trafficked into the Greek trade are re-sold on the
flesh market to pimps in Turkey, the Middle East and throughout Europe. And the main factor behind the trade's astonishing
success "is the corruption. You can't operate illegal enterprises
this big and this complex without corrupt officials."

Dimitris Kyriazidis, president of the Pan Hellenic Confed-
eration of Police Officers, stunned the nation in April 2001
when he publicly acknowledged the involvement of the police
"in networks which traffic illegal women" in Greece. Then
came more international embarrassment.

In July 2001, when the U.S. government waded into the
human trafficking debacle with its first annual worldwide
report card, it ranked twenty-three nations, including Greece,
at the bottom of the barrel. The State Department report
pointed out that Greece had not made significant efforts to
combat trafficking, failed to acknowledge publicly that trafficking is a problem, failed to implement comprehensive
anti-trafficking legislation, rarely prosecuted traffickers and
awarded light sentences to punish traffickers when they were

tried. It also cited corruption in the police and border control as "a major problem."

Not long after this report was released, Human Rights Watch issued a blistering forty-one-page Memorandum of Concern on the problem of trafficking of women in Greece, noting that the trade "often involves the complicity of the police and corrupt immigration officials. In fact, many believe that the international phenomenon of trafficking in women for forced prostitution could not exist at any level without the involvement of such officials."

Greek newspapers have documented numerous incidents of police participation, including the issuing of fake residence and employment permits to women who work illegally under appalling conditions as virtual sex slaves for Greek and Albanian gangs throughout the country. In one embarrassing incident in late October 2000, police in the northern Greek city of Thessalonica raided a strip club suspected of harboring trafficked women. They pulled out six girls. A few hours later the cops discovered that the Tutti Frutti club was a hefty advertiser in the police union's bimonthly magazine.

Two months after that came a screaming headline in the daily *Eleftherotypia:* the police department's Internal Affairs had uncovered a major prostitution procurement ring allegedly run by officers in the central region of Thessaly. According to the leaked confidential report, the operation—known locally as the "meat machine"—had trafficked some 1200 Eastern European women into Greece to work as prostitutes and raked in more than $100 million in criminal proceeds over a ten-year period. Police of varying ranks in the towns of Karditsa and Trikala were involved in the ring, as well as respected business-men, an employee of a prosecutor's office who allegedly tried to extort money from the racket and two personal security guards for an influential Member of Parliament. One of the women purchased and used by the ring told a judge that police officers frequented the club where she worked. By day they would come in uniform to check that the club's papers were in order. They would return at night in street clothes for "gratis" services.

In one particularly scandalous incident, a police officer and a retired cop were arrested during a 1998 raid on an Athens apartment where two Ukrainian women were imprisoned and forced into prostitution. Neighbors told officers with the Aliens Bureau who conducted the covert operation that the women were constantly beaten into submission. Although the neigh-bors had repeatedly complained to the local police station about the screams emanating from the flat, no action was ever taken. The police officer arrested in the raid worked at that station, and investigators found an album containing photographs of the man, often dressed in parts of his uniform, in bed with various young women.

In the 1998 suicide of Irini Penkina cited earlier, police also received several complaints from residents of the apartment building in which she and three other women had been held. All the calls went unanswered. There was even an anonymous phone call to the police station in Thessalonica the day before she killed herself. Again, the police failed to respond. Just a few months earlier, three officers in the same precinct were arrested on charges of protecting prostitution rings in that town.

With every embarrassing scandal, Greek politicians vow to champion a campaign to ferret out the rotten cops and bureaucrats and shut down the illicit flesh trade. In their effort to stem the public furor, they promise swift action and concrete change. A series of stage-managed raids are carried out on known bordellos. Trafficked women are rounded up and deported. Pimps and corrupt police are arrested and charged, and then all goes quiet as the cases end up being mired in the judicial process, which has been described by the U.S. State Department as "slow and inefficient." In Greece, criminal cases usually take just under eighteen months to come to trial, a little before the maximum pretrial detention period expires. It takes an average of eight years for cases to be finally decided. Given the situation, it's no wonder the trafficking trade repeatedly springs back into action once the spotlight is off.

POLICE CORRUPTION is also at the very core of the trafficking trade in Israel. But despite the countless allegations against serving and retired cops, this sordid situation hardly causes a stir in political and government circles. At her tiny office in Tel Aviv, Nomi Levenkron rattled off an alarming number of cases she's documented that expose police involvement.

> I cannot stress enough the widespread phenomenon of bribery among Israeli policemen, many who cooperate freely with pimps and traffickers. Furthermore, many policemen are regular clients of brothels. This keeps many victims from

complaining against their assailants since they see this as cooperation between the assailants and the authorities, leaving them no option of escape.

Sigal Rozen, who heads the Hotline for Migrant Workers in Tel Aviv, said that in some cases police "receive discounts due to their good relations with the brothel owners." She added that "the most extreme cases we know about are those of policemen who were actively involved in buying and selling women or policemen who returned arrested women back to their pimps for a proper amount of money."

Sitting at her desk piled high with files on rescued trafficking victims, Rozen told the story of a young Russian woman named Larissa whom she met in spring 2001 during a visit to the Neveh Tirza prison for women outside Tel Aviv. What alerted her radar was that the authorities were making a special effort to speed up the woman's deportation.

Larissa's story is similar to that of many of the Natashas in Israel. She answered an ad in a local Russian newspaper offering work to young women as au pairs. She contacted the recruiter, who explained that Israeli law forbade her to work in the country legally and that the agency would have to prepare forged documents for her and smuggle her into the country via Egypt. Desperate for a job, Larissa agreed. She was flown to Cairo and transported overland through the Sinai Desert to a desolate area close to the Israeli border. From there, she—along with several other women—was led on foot by Bedouin smugglers to an Israeli border town, where she was picked up by a Russian Jew who drove her to Tel Aviv. Once in the city, Larissa learned her true fate. She was sold to an Israeli pimp who told her she would have to work as a prostitute. According to Rozen,

> When she realized her predicament, she refused to cooperate. She was so beautiful. She was very young and very, very popular. She never accepted her situation to say, "Okay, I came to be an au pair, but I have to earn money to get out of here." She refused to work and was raped repeatedly. She was crying all the time. After a week, the police raided the brothel where she was held. When she was arrested, she told me she was so happy.

Larissa claimed that the police officer who took her into custody escorted her out of the police station, placed her in squad car and drove to Jerusalem where, Rozen said, "He sold her to another pimp for a fistful of dollars."

> She was fully prepared to testify in court about what had happened, but the police, understandably, were not eager to hear her story or launch a full-scale investigation. The police didn't even bother to investigate. They said because she put on a condition that she wanted to stay in Israel if she testified it proved she was lying. How they can arrive at such a conclusion? I don't know. Still, I only had one side of the story, and I never got the police side because they did not want to give one. Larissa was eventually deported and the policeman she accuses of selling her probably still serves in the Israeli police force.

Unrelenting in her mission to stop the traffic in her homeland, Nomi Levenkron made headlines in May 2001 when she filed an unusual petition with the Israeli High Court of Justice.

She asked that it *order* the police to listen to the testimony of four of her clients and to investigate the allegations they were making against their pimps.

"We claimed that the police appear to be systematically ignoring the requests by foreign women who are under detention and want to supply information that might incriminate their Israeli pimps," she said.

The petition also asked that the police explain their approach to trafficked women, bluntly suggesting that their inaction "may be due to the possibility that the owners of the brothels where the women are employed are on friendly terms with police officers, and also to the fact that policemen are among the clients of the brothels. Some policemen come to the brothels for services in uniform."

Levenkron highlighted the case of one of her clients, a twenty-four-year-old Ukrainian woman who was smuggled into Israel in December 2000 from Egypt over the Sinai Desert. She had been promised work as a waitress, but until her arrest in March 2001 she had been forced to work for an escort service in Tel Aviv. Levenkron's petition states:

> She was sold to a procurer for $5000. He employed her in a parlor at 40 Pinsker Street in Tel Aviv seven days a week from 10 a.m. until 5 a.m. the following day, in return for fifteen shekels a day for cigarettes and twenty shekels for food. The women who worked in the apartment were not given the opportunity to leave unless they were accompanied [by a pimp], and when the owners left the apartment, they locked the women inside.

The owners were identified as two brothers, David and Meir. The victim did not know their family name. The petition goes on to say that during the time the Ukrainian woman worked at the brothel "it was constantly visited by policemen in uniform, who seemed to her to be on friendly terms with the owners. David even boasted to the women on a number of occasions that they had no reason to be afraid that they would be arrested, as he had ties with the police that constituted an 'insurance policy' against being arrested." That insurance marker came into play in March 2001, the petition noted, when three of the women who worked in the brothel were arrested but returned later that same day to their pimp.

The lawyer also cited the harrowing experiences of three other women—an eighteen- and a twenty-two-year-old from Moldova, and a twenty-one-year-old Ukrainian. They were all smuggled into Israel overland from Egypt and put to work in a brothel in the town of Be'er Sheva. Over a period of several months, the women were "forced to take an average of eighteen clients a day. When they were not working, they were locked inside the apartment. Among the regular clients were policemen, who showed the women their ID." Moreover, the women "identified the policeman who came to arrest them as a client who had visited the brothel two or three days earlier. The policeman who interrogated them at the station and took their fingerprints visited the brothel, as a client, on the morning of the arrest."

All the cases cited in the petition became moot with the deportation of the women.

On several occasions Levenkron raised the issue of policemen visiting brothels as clients to the chief of police, as well as to the commander of the division that investigates police conduct at the Ministry of Justice. "The answer was always the same: there is nothing to be done. Although this behavior might not become a policeman, it is still not a crime."

THE CONTEMPTIBLE ACTIONS of even the lowliest of bureaucrats can have dramatic repercussions. This was the case with a particularly nasty trafficking network that had its genesis in Prague, the capital of the Czech Republic, and reached into the United States.

One hazy August morning in 1996, Michael Bayer, a strapping six-foot-one special agent with the visa fraud section, U.S. State Department Bureau of Diplomatic Security in Washington, sat back at his desk, switched on the computer and saw he had mail. It was an urgent dispatch from a security officer at the American embassy in Prague: a Czech police officer had visited the embassy the day before with a tip about a gang of thugs smuggling young women into the United States.

Bayer promptly wrote back that he'd see what he could find out on his side of the ocean. But before he could fire off any queries he got another email the very next day from the anti-fraud section of consular affairs in Washington. Its job is to monitor immigration fraud trends targeting the U.S. That email alerted him to the recent arrival of a number of young, single Czech women at New York's Kennedy Airport. They had valid U.S. entry visas, but there was something suspicious about the travel documents. They were all filled out in a very similar manner—a telltale sign of fraud.

"That, with the other tip, well, bang, zoom, I knew something was going on," the agent recounted.

Bayer's investigation kicked into overdrive. The consular section in Prague started pulling all the visa applications in a hunt for a pattern. It wasn't long before they found it.

"All these applications were filled out with a common destination in New York City, which was a hotel up around 10th Avenue and 49th Street, kind of the seedier side of Times Square," Bayer said. "It was an area known for prostitution. So it was pretty clear that we had a prostitution ring going straight into New York City."

The area was staked out by a team of undercover cops, but nothing came of it.

"It was busy and we really couldn't tell who was doing what. There were so many people around. So that didn't really work out that well. But we knew young Czech women were coming into the States and where they were going once they got here."

Intelligence amassed by Czech police revealed that the women were departing Prague in groups of three or four at a time, and that over a four-year period as many as 200 may have been illegally smuggled into New York.

"We actually saw some of the groups coming in and pretty soon it became clear who was involved and what was going on," Bayer said.

Two Czech expatriates named Ladislav Ruc and Milan Lejhanec were meeting the women at Kennedy Airport. Ruc, then thirty-eight, was the mastermind. He was a big man who enjoyed playing the role of a Mafia don. His look was intimidating. A body-builder buff, he wore his gel-slicked hair in a ponytail. He dressed in skin-tight T-shirts, cowboy boots, cheesy sharkskin suits and flashy jewelry. On one occasion, he arrived at a Czech wedding in Queens in a Rolls-Royce chauffeured by Lejhanec, his trusted lieutenant. Lejhanec was very much the lackey. At twenty-seven, he was a career criminal with a record in the Czech Republic for transporting stolen cars. He was also convicted for attempting to sell plastique explosives that had been stolen from an army storage depot. There were a number of other Czech expatriates in the gang, but Ruc was the ringleader.

With the key players identified and the pattern established, Bayer decided it was time to turn up the heat and asked the New York police for assistance.

"They fixed me up with some vice cops in lower Manhattan who were also organized crime cops. They were the cream of their crop. I started telling them the background of this thing when a detective cuts in and says, 'You know what, I just arrested a woman for prostitution who I think ran away from this same gang.'"

The agent jotted down the particulars and set up a meeting.

She was really pissed at these guys and she was more than willing to talk about the whole set-up and give details about who did what. Finding her was the real break in the case because she provided so much meat, so much juice for the taking. The only problem with her was she was so terrified of these guys because they're big and they're scary and they're mean. She truly believed they would kill someone for $500. So it became important for me to try to work with her as much as I could and get her to try to direct me to some other girls, because now I had one witness but that wasn't enough.

What Bayer learned from his Jane Doe was the inner workings of the gang's criminal enterprise. She described how the women were recruited through ads placed in local Czech newspapers for dancers, waitresses and models. They were met by the recruiters at the main train station in Wenceslas Square in Prague. The women didn't have to venture into the U.S. embassy with a concocted story and hope for the best—the gang members simply directed them to a specific employee in the visa section who rubber-stamped their applications. Within days they were bound for New York. Ruc and Lejhanec picked them up at the airport and took them to one of three cockroach- and rat-infested apartments in Queens, where the women lived out of their suitcases and slept on mattresses on the floor.

The women were immediately put to work in grueling ten-hour shifts at peep-show parlors near Times Square. The main two were the Playpen—a narrow, sleazy bar with blacked-out windows at street level—and the Playground, on the second floor above a hard-core porn shop on Eighth Avenue and packed with peep-show stalls.

"I was told by vice cops that the Playpen and Playground used to be notorious for having drug addicts, the real kind of bottom-of-the-barrel type of product," Bayer recounted. "Then they said these two places started getting all these beautiful

Czech women and other beautiful foreign women coming in, and all of a sudden they're raking in the dough."

At the peep-show parlors customers would enter a closet-like room and feed quarters into a slot. A motorized metal screen would rise for about a minute before dropping down. In a flesh pit on the other side were naked women. For a price, the voyeurs could reach in and grope them. But before they touched, the girls were required to ask for a tip.

"That was the kind of the language for the transaction," Bayer explained. "Well, there was an actual price for touching each part of the body. Sort of like a meat chart. The going price was $2 for the breast, $3 for the buttock and $5 for genital contact. So the customer would reach through the hole in this peep-show booth and that's how contact was made."

Under New York law, this sort of sexual activity is illegal and falls under the statute dealing with prostitution. However, the club owners figured they could get away with it by instructing the women not to charge a fee but to ask for a gratuity.

> Whatever the girls made in tips, they had to give a cut to Milan and Larry [Ruc]. And the going rate of these guys is $100 a day per girl, and she has to pay that six days a week. You could imagine if you're getting pawed for $2 and $3 at a time, it takes a lot to make $100 a day. So there's either a lot of extra activity going on or there's a heck of a lot of activity going on in these peep shows.

While Bayer built his case against Ruc and Lejhanec, the investigation in the Republic zeroed in on the crooked embassy employee—a female Czech national. American investigators, with help from the Czech police, set up a sting to nail her.

"We sent in a young Czech policewoman pretending to be one of these women clients and it worked beautifully," Bayer said. "The employee confessed right away when confronted and agreed to cooperate with our investigation. She told us she alone issued more than a hundred visas for $100 apiece. She was hoping to make enough money to buy a bar in Prague."

Her information led to the arrest of a number of key players in the Czech Republic, including Lejhanec's mother and brother and a "businessman" who operated out of the town of Partibitsa about an hour outside Prague.

"This was the actual center they worked out of and recruited women," Bayer explained. "What they were doing there was placing advertisements in one of the Czech national newspapers for waitresses, models and nannies."

Back in New York, the agent pressed forward with the case.

"As time goes on—and this thing is going on over a lot of months—I'm asking my primary contact to fix me up with other girls who've run away. So over a period of a year she leads me to three others. So now I have four women telling me the same stories."

The takedown was set for March 12, 1998. A team of officers from the NYPD, the State Department diplomatic security and the Immigration and Naturalization Service (INS) hit the Playpen and Playground.

"We had 150 cops and agents ready to roll. We had good knowledge of the best time to raid—that was, believe it or not, around five o'clock, at rush hour when all the businessmen got out of work. That's where a lot of them go before they head home to their families."

The raids recovered thirty-nine women from the Czech Republic and Hungary. Apparently another gang, headed by a thug named Zoltan, was handling the Hungarian trade. In the club offices the police found $250,000 in cash, along with drugs and a few handguns.

> We also got hold of a whole bunch of contracts for these women and on them were pictures of them and their visas. It was all really good stuff, and in addition there was a big sign in the women's locker room of the prices that they were to charge for these different parts of their body. This was direct evidence. Now we had a big price list from the locker room and we had sixteen good witnesses from this raid itself and we had a good history of what was going on.

Arrest teams also went after the two main suspects in Queens. They nailed Lejhanec at his home and found a cache of weapons—Russian- and Israeli-made automatic pistols—as well as passports, visas, airline tickets and a ledger detailing the money taken from each of the women. Ruc wasn't home at the time but police found a pile of incriminating evidence. A few days later, the gang leader turned himself in.

> From that point to about June 1998, we compiled and cross-referenced all the evidence. We interviewed all the witnesses and established seven that were really good. Not only that, we had the work contracts, airline ticket invoices, the INS

data of when they entered the country and all their visas. So I had a great document trail that clearly implicated this gang in the Czech Republic and the United States. I had them coming and going. They were toast.

At their trial in June 1999, Ruc and Lejhanec pled guilty and were each sentenced to sixty months in prison with an order that they be deported as soon as they completed their time. Still, five years for trafficking and brutalizing so many innocent women is hardly a deterrent. The court could have sent a much stronger message, one that would make traffickers think twice about getting into this business. As for their victims, most were deported or returned, disgraced, to their homes in the Czech Republic.

STORIES OF SYSTEMIC COMPLICITY, complacency and corruption abound on the trafficking scene worldwide. It is a wonder sometimes that any women are rescued at all. And when they are, most are treated as whores. The reason is simple: if a cop were to admit that he'd used any of these women, he'd also have to face the fact that he's guilty of rape.

To most trafficked women the "enemy" includes police, border guards and immigration officers. But there is yet another formidable foe among those in uniform: military men. In war-torn regions under control of UN peacekeepers and U.S. soldiers the words "democracy" and "peace" ring hollow for thousands of trafficked women imprisoned in bars and brothels adjacent to military bases. In these far-flung, out-of-sight hovels, fifteen-year-old girls are fair game . . . and rape is just another word for rest and recreation.

BOSNIAN
NIGHTS

We had a Christmas party where they had all these
slaves there. One guy brought three girls to the party.
—BENJAMIN JOHNSTON, A FORMER DYNCORP WORKER
HIRED TO REPAIR HELICOPTERS AT A U.S. MILITARY BASE

IN DECEMBER 1995, in the wake of a brutal forty-two-month
war against Serbian-led forces, more than 50,000 NATO
peacekeepers marched into Bosnia and Herzegovina to
restore law and order. A number of Serbian fighters were
rounded up, charged with rape and sent to The Hague to
stand trial for war crimes. But in the peacetime that followed,
thousands of women and girls—abducted from Eastern Europe
and forced to work as sex slaves in the bars and brothels that dot
the mountainous Bosnian countryside—became fair game for

the tens of thousands of UN peacekeepers and international aid workers who poured into the region. The irony is ugly. During war, the rape of innocent women and children by soldiers is deemed a heinous war crime. During peacetime, it's a different story.

OLENKA, A NINETEEN-YEAR-OLD UKRAINIAN, sits across from me in a coffee shop chain-smoking cigarettes. She is tall and thin, her skin is pale and her dyed-blond hair cropped short. She stares nervously down at her ruby red fingernails as she recounts her six-month descent into hell as a sex slave in a bar in the northern Bosnian town of Tulza. Olenka was just seventeen at the time, but the nightmares still haunt her. She takes a long drag from a cigarette and begins her story.

"I went with between eight and fifteen men a night. I did not want to have sex with any of them. If I did not do as I was told, my owner said I would be beaten to death. This man was cruel and vicious. You did not cross him."

In the months she was held captive, Olenka figures she was raped more than 1800 times. The men each paid the owner $50. She never saw a penny. On one particularly harrowing evening she was passed around to a dozen soldiers. The men were rambunctious, celebrating a birthday in the bar. One of their buddies had turned twenty-one. She was the birthday present . . . for the entire platoon. Whatever the peacekeepers wanted, she was forced to give.

"The entire time, I must smile and make them believe I am enjoying this humiliation," Olenka said in a barely audible whisper. "These men were animals. They cared nothing that I was there as a prisoner. They simply wanted sex."

She doesn't know the names of any of the men who used her over that period, but she remembers the uniforms and the insignias emblazoned on their shoulders—American, Canadian, British, Russian, French. Many were soldiers. Some were police officers with the UN. Others were among the thousands of workers—with either the myriad international agencies or the UN—that flooded the region after the conflict. Many times, she would plead for help. Some of her international "patrons" had cell phones dangling from their belts. She asked them to let her make just one call.

"They all refused. All they cared about was they had bought me for the hour and I was there for their pleasure. One of them told the owner I asked to use his cell phone. For that, I was beaten and left in a cellar without food for three days."

When Olenka was finally arrested in a raid on the bar, she recognized eight of her "clients" among the police who carried out the bust. Some were with the UN International Police Task Force (IPTF); others were with the local police. After her arrest she was interviewed by an international human rights worker. "I told her about the soldiers, the police officers and the internationals, but nothing ever came of it."

Two weeks later Olenka was sent home—penniless, shattered and in disgrace. For the UN Mission in Bosnia-Herzegovina (UNMIBH), however, she numbers among the statistics as yet another trafficked woman "saved" by the IPTF.

PROSTITUTION IS ILLEGAL in Bosnia, but since the war it has skyrocketed. Throughout this tiny region, population 3.5 million, there are now more than 260 bars. They're really brothels, housing up to 5000 Eastern European women who've become nothing more than playthings for the international soldiers and staff. Many of the very people entrusted with bringing stability to this region have resorted to what would, within their own borders, have them charged with complicity, corruption, abetting trafficking, sexual assault and rape. None of this nocturnal activity is news to the UN brass; they've tried desperately to keep a tight lid on it. That lid was blown off on October 9, 2000, by a thirty-nine-year-old mother of three from Nebraska.

Kathryn Bolkovac was one of 2100 police officers serving with the IPTF in Bosnia-Herzegovina. The force was created to help restore law and order after the war and train a new breed of officers to police the region. Bolkovac signed a three-year contract to work with the IPTF in 1998. For her it was the opportunity of a lifetime—a chance to travel abroad and to do something meaningful. Her placement was arranged by DynCorp Inc., which hires American police officers on behalf of the U.S. State Department to serve in UN missions around the world. DynCorp, headquartered in Reston, Virginia, was contracted to provide up to 300 IPTF officers in Bosnia-Herzegovina.

Soon after she arrived in Sarajevo, Bolkovac was asked to run the IPTF's Gender Office—a unit handling a wide variety of offenses and investigations, including sex trafficking, sexual assault and domestic abuse. In no time at all, she found herself swamped with trafficking cases. One of her jobs was to interview rescued women, and it was during these sessions that the officer began to notice an alarming trend. Time and time again the young women revealed that peacekeepers, UN workers and international police frequented the brothels where they had been forced to work. Yet, strangely enough, each time Bolkovac filed a report it disappeared, unacknowledged, into a black hole.

She decided to take matters into her own hands. On October 9, 2000, she snapped the chain of command and fired off an explosive email to more than fifty people in senior positions—including Jacques Klein, the UN secretary-general's special representative in Bosnia. Entitled "Not to be read by those with a weak stomach or guilty feelings," her missive charged that NATO soldiers, humanitarian workers and UN police were regular customers of bars where Eastern European women—some as young as fifteen—were being held.

Based on her interviews with more than eighty of these women, Bolkovac described the rape, torture and humiliation they endured on a daily basis. "If the women refuse to perform sex acts with the customers they are beaten and raped in the rooms by the bar owners and their associates." She didn't mince words. Frequenting these brothels was akin to aiding and abetting "sexual slavery," she wrote. But that wasn't the worst of it. IPTF officers were also *facilitating* trafficking, in more ways than one—forging documents for trafficked women, aiding their illegal transport into Bosnia and tipping off bar owners about impending raids. Lest her allegations be dismissed as generalization, Bolkovac offered up a few specifics. An American police officer had bought one of these women for $1000 and had kept her locked in his apartment, using her on a whim for his sexual pleasure. In another case, a NATO peacekeeper was intercepted by local police as he tried to enter the region with four Moldovan women in his car. When the women were questioned by the IPTF, they said they were "brought across the border illegally, sold and forced into prostitution."

Within days, Bolkovac was removed from front-line policing and banished to a telex room in a Sarajevo suburb, far from trafficked women and investigative police work. Her boss, Mike Stiers, who was then deputy commissioner of the IPTF, claimed she had been reassigned for behaving unprofessionally in her quest to help trafficked women. What's more, he noted, she had lost sight of the main priority of the IPTF—ending the ethnic violence that threatened to unravel the country's fragile peace.

Stiers was immediately confronted by Madeleine Rees, head of the UN Office of the High Commissioner for Human Rights in Sarajevo. Rees, a lawyer and human rights activist, maintains that what happened to Bolkovac was wrong. "He told me that 'she's burnt out. She's too close to the issue. We need a more objective picture.'" Rees countered that Bolkovac was a good investigator who simply wanted to get something done. "When she tried to raise the issue with the command, she got no backing," Rees recalled. "The attitude was, Why are you wasting so much time on these whores?"

Less than a year later, Bolkovac was fired for allegedly fabricating her timesheets. This, the police officer avows, was blatantly false; she was being punished for breaking the chain of command. "I was driven out," Bolkovac said, "because I was outspoken on this issue."

Upon leaving Sarajevo, she sought legal advice and filed a complaint against DynCorp before a labor tribunal in Southampton, England. The evidence at the hearing painted an ugly picture of the very people who, as she says, were sent to the region to help. Bolkovac testified that "the victims of trafficking were reporting extensive use of the brothels and other criminal acts by the international community and international police task forces." In Bolkovac's view, the reason behind her eventual dismissal was clear.

DynCorp held that the dismissal had nothing to do with her email. It also denied turning a blind eye to its employees' inappropriate behavior. In fact, the company argued that it always took "swift action" whenever it learned of "moral misconduct by a U.S. police officer." It noted that in November and December 2000, after Bolkovac's allegations first surfaced, it had fired two officers for "participation in prostitution" and one for purchasing a trafficking victim and forcing her to live with him for six months to provide sexual services.

Perhaps the most damaging testimony before the tribunal was the description of how trafficked women are viewed in the eyes of international police. Bolkovac said that her supervisor, Mike Stiers, had flippantly dismissed trafficked women as "just prostitutes," leading many officers in the mission to believe it was acceptable to frequent the brothels where these women were held. Her evidence was bolstered by Madeleine Rees, who described how officers working in Bosnia believed investigations into the use of prostitutes were "inhibiting their freedom." According to Rees, "They almost always referred to the trafficked women as 'whores seeking a free ride home' . . . I know of these opinions first-hand since this was also the attitude of those in very senior positions."

Rees rocked the tribunal when she testified that a top UN official was spotted at the bar of one of the most notorious brothels in Bosnia. She said that one of the women held at the brothel had identified American Dennis Laducer, a deputy commissioner of the IPTF, as a patron. (Laducer is no longer involved with the organization; his employment records state that he should never work for the United Nations again.) Rees boldly accused the UN of failing to properly deal with officers who were sexually abusing women. Bolkovac, whom she described as having "absolute integrity," was the only person confronting the issue. "I am in no doubt Kathy was taken out of the mission because she confronted the issue of trafficking," she told the tribunal.

The tribunal agreed. In a searing twenty-one-page judgment, it ruled that Bolkovac had been unfairly dismissed. Tribunal chairman Charles Twiss concluded that "there is no doubt whatever that the reason for her dismissal was that she made a protected disclosure" when she sent the email.

Bolkovac wasn't the only one to run into the infamous "blue wall," nor was she the only one in Bosnia to meet with resistance while investigating the behavior of the international police. David Lamb, a former police officer from Philadelphia, had also signed up with DynCorp for a three-year stint with the IPTF in Bosnia-Herzegovina. By February 2001 he was working as a human rights investigator in central Bosnia. In the course of one investigation, Lamb happened upon a group of trafficked women rescued in a raid. They described how a Romanian IPTF officer and his wife were directly involved in the recruitment and sale of women to a brothel in the Bosnian town of Zvornik. Like Bolkovac, Lamb dug deeper, and like Bolkovac, he was stunned by what he learned.

Within weeks, his investigation turned up more than enough evidence to justify a full-scale criminal investigation. He discovered that IPTF members were directly linked to forcing girls into prostitution. In one case, two Romanian IPTF cops were said to have recruited Romanian women. They purchased false travel documents for them, smuggled them into Bosnia and sold them to local bar owners to work as prostitutes.

The story—which started out like Bolkovac's—seemed to be repeating itself, but this time Lamb's team was explicitly warned not to dig too deep. At one point a senior IPTF officer ordered them to end the investigation altogether. Other times, they were pulled aside by colleagues and threatened with physical harm if they pursued the matter. Pablo Bradie, a police officer from Argentina who had been assigned to Lamb's investigative team, described in an internal memo dated March 18, 2001, how one Romanian IPTF officer admitted to buying travel documents for two women. At the same time, the officer warned Bradie: "Stop immediately anything against the Romanians. Do not mess with me, neither with my colleague . . . I will not tell you more, but I think you can guess what will happen."

Lamb refused to back down. A week and a half later he sent an email to the IPTF command, identifying five UN police officers "linked to allegations of involvement in prostitution and women trafficking." In it, he pointed out that whenever investigations uncovered UN involvement, support from UN headquarters coincidentally dried up. But that wasn't all. "During investigations by my office into UN personnel involvement in women trafficking, my investigators and I experienced an astonishing cover-up attempt that seemed to extend to the highest levels of the UN headquarters."

Lamb's tenure with the IPTF ended in April 2001. There was no attempt to extend his contract, and he was sent packing back to Philadelphia. The investigation was turned over to Rosario Ioanna, a Canadian member of the IPTF. Ioanna picked up where Lamb left off, compiling a list of about a dozen Romanian officers said to frequent brothels. But he too faced an uphill battle: according to a confidential report prepared by the investigative team for the UN Internal Affairs Section, Romanian officers tried to impede Ioanna's investigation by attempting to remove four trafficked women from police custody and intimidating them during questioning. Like Lamb, Ioanna was learning that some of the officers were doing more than just frequenting brothels. In one instance, a Romanian police officer was given a tractor to work his family farm back home. In return, he was using inside information to tip off brothel owners about impending raids.

By this time the UN mission understood it was facing a colossal problem. In the span of eighteen months, the IPTF's own investigators had shone a spotlight on police involvement in prostitution and trafficking. Some of the top UN brass began pushing for an independent inquiry, among them Mary Robinson, the UN's high commissioner for Human Rights in Geneva. At Robinson's insistence, the UN Office of Internal Oversight (OIO) sent two investigators from New York to conduct a preliminary inquiry. The investigators arrived on June 26, 2001, and less than two weeks later they reported their findings. Fred Eckhard, chief spokesperson for the UN, announced, "They did not find any evidence of systematic or organized involvement in human trafficking." Eckhard did, however, concede that the OIO crew had offered a number of recommendations on "how the UN police could strengthen their role in combating human trafficking."

The announcement was met with astonishment by most human rights observers on the ground in Bosnia. Madeleine Rees was appalled. She wondered how the OIO investigators could have arrived at such a quick and unequivocal conclusion, considering that "they never once ventured out of the UN building in Sarajevo . . . They said they had complete access to the files. But there was nothing in them." They did *not* contact the IPTF investigators who had voiced the concerns—such as Bolkovac and Lamb. They did *not* interview any of the rescued women who had made the allegations in the first place. They did *not* speak to any of the international police officers who had been accused of trafficking in women, and they did not even read what Rees later described as a very telling and crucial internal report that had been prepared by Internal Affairs at the UN office in Sarajevo:

> I saw that report. It dealt with serious offenses that warranted investigation. It raised serious doubts about the UN delegation here and it contained allegations of a Romanian IPTF cop and his wife running a brothel here. When that was brought to the attention of the investigators, they said that their mandate was to determine whether there was widespread systemic abuse, and for that, they said they had all the information they needed for a proper and thorough investigation.

So why was the UN's own report ignored? Perhaps the answer lies in what the OIO investigators were sent to do. In the course of their investigation they had met with Rees: "They told me they were here to disprove Kathryn Bolkovac's allegations."

For Jacques Klein, head of the UN mission in Bosnia, the OIO's conclusions were a clear vindication. They weren't at all convincing, though, and the word "cover-up" began reverberating down corridors of his own mission. Klein responded by issuing a press release in which he trumpeted his success. First, he boasted of having implemented a "zero-tolerance policy toward sexual or other serious misconduct." He went on to concede that on a number of occasions, individual officers had been sent home: "The ultimate sanction against offenders is removal from UN service and repatriation to their home countries . . . This has been the fate of 24 international police officers, among them eight Americans." The admission, however, was tempered by a warm tribute to the 10,000 police officers who had served with the IPTF since 1996: "The vast majority have performed in a highly professional manner and to the great credit of their home countries and the United States."

As to the real issue at hand, Klein was brief: "I can assure you that during my tenure there have been no cover-ups." He stressed that the allegations against DynCorp and American IPTF officers had been investigated not only by the OIO but also by the U.S. State Department itself. "All have reached the same conclusion," he proclaimed, "namely, that the allegations could not be substantiated."

Then came the clincher. Klein griped that shining a negative spotlight on UN peacekeepers was *interfering* with the real problem at hand. "Placing undue and unfair emphasis on UN peacekeepers diverts attention away from those ultimately responsible for trafficking. The focus of our efforts should be on corrupt government officials and members of organized crime who perpetrate the trade and allow it to flourish."

This very mindset was undoubtedly behind the spectacle that had unfolded just a year earlier, when a raid on three brothels in the town of Prijedor in northern Bosnia quickly escalated from a goodwill rescue to a public relations nightmare.

WITH THE IPTF STILL REELING over Bolkovac's incendiary email and with its force under a black cloud of suspicion, the UN command needed to show that it was serious about trafficking. The solution: a high-profile raid. On November 13, 2000, the IPTF hit three clubs in Prijedor. The bars, known to be holding trafficked women, were called Crazy Horse 1, Crazy Horse 2 and Masquerade. Two days later the UN proclaimed its success in a press release: "This was the most significant police action taken to date by police in Bosnia and Herzegovina to address the serious problem of human trafficking and forced prostitution." Thirty-three of the women rescued from the clubs were "victims of human trafficking for the purpose of forced prostitution." The women were from Romania, Moldova, Russia and Ukraine. Several were believed to be as young as fourteen.

One week later, after all the congratulatory slaps on the back, the raids were about to make the news again. This time, however, the key player wasn't the IPTF but rather the owner of the bars, Milorad Milakovic, who had been arrested during the raids and charged with inducing women into prostitution. Milakovic decided to call a press conference of his own on the outskirts of the town of Banjaluka, not far from Prijedor. Banjaluka had its own press club, but Milakovic staged his spectacle at the side of a dirt road. The reason, he explained to the gathered newshounds, was that the local police had barred him from entering the town.

The press conference itself was a curious sight. Several thuggish-looking men wearing black leather jackets milled about on the road. They carried homemade signs, giving the event the feel of a union walkout. One of the placards was directed at the international police—an unimaginative

"IPTF GO HOME." Another singled out a particular cop: "DAVID IS NOT A PEACEKEEPER BUT A PERVERT."

Milakovic, a former cop, stood officiously in the middle of the rabble, flanked by his wife and son, along with two "dancers" from his clubs by the names of Kristina and Lujz. With an indignant air, he launched into his spiel. First, he attacked the IPTF, claiming that six of its officers were regular patrons at his bars, and some were among the squad that had raided them the week before. But that wasn't all. According to the businessman, the raids weren't "rescues"; they were *retribution*.

Then Milakovic dropped a bomb. He had been asked, he said, to pay $10,000 in bribes to certain IPTF officers, and when he refused his bars were raided in direct retaliation. He cited one officer in particular—the "David" whose name was plastered on the placards carried around by his goons. David had demanded not only protection money in monthly installments but also free access to his female dancers for sex. Milakovic revealed that he had audiotapes and eyewitnesses to corroborate his claim.

UN officials in Sarajevo dismissed Milakovic as a lunatic hell-bent on revenge . . . but the allegations, damaging as they were, were never actually denied.

The following day brought more bad news when the "good news" raids hit the spotlight again. Although the original UN press release had said the raids had been carried out by local Prijedor police monitored by members of the IPTF, a high-ranking official with the Bosnian government now pointed out that they didn't involve *any* local police. The implication was clear: rather than "monitoring," the IPTF had actually staged and carried out the raid. This was in direct contravention of the IPTF's mandate—which was to assist and supervise—and it flew in the face of the UN's own procedures and regulations, which required that all raids be conducted by local police.

Reporters smelled a rat and went on the hunt for Alun Roberts, the official IPTF spokesman for Banjaluka. For two days Roberts was nowhere to be found. When he finally surfaced, he was peppered with questions to which his only response was a terse "No comment." He refused to confirm or deny the existence of "David."

It didn't take long, however, for reporters to figure out who David was. According to UN police sources, he wasn't a commander but a regular IPTF cop. He was of Irish descent and was either British or American. It was rumored that he loved beautiful women, booze and brawls. After the scandal broke, the elusive David disappeared from Prijedor and soon after vanished from Bosnia altogether. Several other IPTF cops involved in the raid also grabbed a cab to the airport. In late November, Roberts resurfaced and read a carefully worded statement. While he refused to name the officers, he announced that a number of them had been sent home. "The six were removed for exceeding their duties in the UN mandate and . . . for inappropriate behavior and violation of the UN mission code of conduct."

Madeleine Rees had no doubt that this "inappropriate behavior" involved frequenting brothels. Rees herself had interviewed the thirty-three women who had been pulled from the clubs after the raid. The girls told her that they had "regularly" had sex with the IPTF cops.

And if the six who were sent home got off easily, Milakovic too received only a slap on the wrist. A few weeks after the raid, he was back in business.

WHILE THE UN MISSION IN SARAJEVO was desperately trying to scrub away the tarnish, yet another sex trafficking scandal was brewing in Bosnia, this time on the civilian side of the peace effort. The controversy involved American workers hired by DynCorp to repair Apache and Blackhawk helicopters at a U.S. military base near the northern town of Tuzla. It didn't come to light until the next year, in June 2000, after DynCorp fired another one of its employees. Two months later, in Fort Worth, Texas, aircraft mechanic Benjamin Johnston sued the company.

Johnston claimed he was canned because he had blown the whistle on the raucous nocturnal activities of some of his American colleagues. According to the lawsuit, Johnston witnessed co-workers and supervisors "buying and selling women for their own personal enjoyment," some even bragging about "the various ages and talents of the individual slaves they had purchased." The main reason he had been fired, he said, was "to preserve the status quo of DynCorp in Bosnia" as well as "the sanctioned buying and selling of women, minor girls, firearms, forged passports and frequent trips to whorehouses."

As Johnston and his legal team prepared to enter the courthouse on the first day of trial in early August 2002, DynCorp quietly settled the lawsuit.

I spoke with Johnston just before the settlement from his home in Lubbock, Texas. He was still shocked and disturbed by what he had seen in Bosnia, and openly shared his side of the story.

He had been stationed in Illisheim, Germany, with the U.S. Army when he was approached by a DynCorp recruiter. The recruiter described the company's many career opportunities, including the chance to contribute to peacemaking missions abroad. The offer was tempting. And so in early 1999 Johnston received an honorable discharge and, on the same day, signed up to work for DynCorp in Bosnia. He was sent to Comanche Base Camp outside Tuzla, where his job involved the maintenance of military aircraft. Within months, the hulking six-foot-five Texan stumbled on a disturbing trend.

"I would see these very young girls walking around town with older guys I worked with," Johnston recalled. "These men would have their hands all over these girls . . . Everybody in the hangar would say, 'I've got this girl and that girl.' At first I didn't know these girls were being bought as slaves, but the longer I stayed, the more I learned what was really going on." His voice breaking in anger, Johnston recounted one particularly upsetting event.

We had a Christmas party where they had all these slaves there. One guy brought three girls to the party. One was putting food in his mouth, the other was pouring his drinks, the other was lighting his cigarettes. He asked all the guys to call him Pimp Daddy. In fact, he had a financial interest in a brothel called Atlantis, and he would brag about going to Serbia and getting the women.

These guys would say, "I gotta go to Serbia this weekend to pick up three girls." They just talked about it like it was so cool and then bragged about how much they paid for them—usually between $600 and $800. The longer I stayed in Bosnia the worse these men acted. They would talk about locking the girls up in their apartments when they went to work so they couldn't escape. Then one day I heard a DynCorp employee brag that his girl wasn't a day over twelve.

Johnston approached the men and told them what they were doing was "just plain wrong." When they ignored him he went to his boss, DynCorp's site manager, John Hirtz. "He told me not to worry about it. He said, 'You can't control what Americans do in their off time.' He just told me to mind my own business . . . At the time, I didn't realize how deep into it he was."

With some digging, the former soldier learned that the girls were being smuggled into Bosnia from Eastern Europe by the Serbian Mafia. They were bought and sold, along with their forged passports, by some of his co-workers and supervisors for $1000 to $1500 each. The DynCorp employees kept their purchased women locked in their apartments for their sexual pleasure.

"This one guy, he was about 400 pounds, just the hugest guy you could imagine," Johnston said. "He had this girl who was just a child, and it just breaks your heart seeing this fifteen-year-old with this man . . . You could see in her face—she was dying." On one occasion, Johnston and his wife had invited a co-worker over to their home for dinner. "The man was in his sixties and he arrives with a fourteen-year-old girl. My wife was just appalled."

Although he had been told repeatedly to butt out, Johnston voiced his concerns to management. But "all stayed the same in DynCorp's little Bosnian Boys' Club," and in no time, Johnston was completely shut out. "The guys just stopped talking to me. I was ousted, shunned. I was one of the few people with an aviation mechanic's license, highly skilled and highly trained. In the end, they had me washing aircraft because I wasn't part of the boys' club."

Ashamed and frustrated that he couldn't get DynCorp management to bring the hammer down on its wayward employees, he turned to the Criminal Investigation Division (CID) of the U.S. Army. Johnston and his wife, Denisa, were immediately placed in protective custody for fear of retaliation by the Serbian Mafia and DynCorp employees. During the investigation Johnston worked closely with the CID, even though it put him at considerable risk. "I drove around with the CID investigators, pointing out everyone's houses who owned women and showing them the DynCorp vans parked outside the whorehouses all night."

In early 2000 the CID, backed by military police, raided the DynCorp hangar. The evidence seized included a pornographic video handed over to military investigators by Kevin Werner, a DynCorp employee. In a sworn statement, Werner admitted to buying a Romanian woman to "rescue" her from prostitution. He also fingered other DynCorp employees who had purchased their own women. The most damaging evidence was the videotape, which featured DynCorp site supervisor John Hirtz. The amateur home-videotape captures Hirtz gleefully having sex with two trafficked women. One of the women is clearly resisting, and he's not taking no for an answer.

Hirtz had made the video but Werner had secretly dubbed a copy for himself as insurance. "I told him I had a copy and that all I wanted was to be treated fairly. If I was going to be fired or laid off, I wanted it to be because of my work performance and not because he wasn't happy with me."

CID investigators then moved in on Hirtz, the one who had first told Johnston to mind his own business. According to a transcript of the interrogation, the investigator asked Hirtz if he had sex with the second woman on the tape.

"Yes," Hirtz replied.

"Did you have intercourse with the second woman after she said no to you?"

"I don't recall her saying that. I don't think it was her saying no."

"Who do you think said no?"

"I don't know."

The investigator replayed the tape.

"According to what you witnessed on the videotape played for you in which you were having sexual intercourse with the second woman, did you have sexual intercourse with the second woman after she said no to you?" the investigator asked again.

"Yes," the DynCorp manager replied.

"Did you know you were being videotaped?"

"Yes. I set it up," Hirtz admitted.

"Did you know it is wrong to force yourself upon someone without their consent?"

"Yes," Hirtz said.

Despite the admission and the evidence against him, no criminal action was ever taken. In fact, none of the men who were purchasing these women faced any criminal sanctions whatsoever. In late June 2002, the CID simply closed the case.

DynCorp, however, fired three of its employees—Hirtz, Werner and, incredibly, Johnston. His termination letter said he was being let go for bringing "discredit to the company and the U.S. Army." Eight months later, in a deposition for the lawsuit, Jonathan Lyons, the DynCorp supervisor who had signed the letter, testified that Johnston had been dismissed because of unverifiable statements he had made to the CID about fellow employees.

In DynCorp's defense, spokeswoman Charlene A. Wheeless argued that it was unfair to blacken the company's reputation because a few employees "behaved inexcusably." Wheeless vehemently rejected any culpability, either in relation to the activity in Bosnia or to Johnston's alleged wrongful dismissal:

> The notion that a company such as DynCorp would turn a blind eye to illegal behavior by our employees is incomprehensible. DynCorp adheres to a core set of values that has served as the backbone of our corporation for the last fifty-five years, helping us become one of the largest and most respected professional-services and outsourcing companies in the world. We can't stress strongly enough that . . . we take

ethics very seriously. DynCorp stands by its decision to terminate Ben Johnston, who was terminated for cause.

Understandably, Johnston is dismayed at how the entire episode turned out.

> They've been trashing my name ever since they found out I blew the whistle. DynCorp makes it sound like it was one or two bad apples but that wasn't the case. It was a big joke over there that you couldn't get in trouble. You had diplomatic immunity and you could do whatever you want, and that's exactly how the guys acted.
>
> There were about forty employees at the base and I would say 75 percent were involved in this . . . They absolutely knew these women were trafficked. They took pride in that. I don't know how DynCorp could find that many immoral people. These guys were the worst diplomats America could ever want overseas.

His voice choked with emotion, Johnston recalled what it was like when the Americans first arrived in Bosnia. "The people were so happy to see them. Then they saw how they acted and asked me, 'Are all Americans like that? Do they like to buy girls in America?' They couldn't believe we didn't have a brothel in every town. I told them it wasn't like that. They thought I was the exception."

ON APRIL 24, 2002, David Lamb sat before the members of the U.S. Congress House Committee on International Relations.

In a measured tone he began his testimony, recalling what he had learned as a human rights investigator in Bosnia.

"UN peacekeepers' participation in the sex slave trade in Bosnia is a significant, widespread problem. More precisely, the sex slave trade in Bosnia largely exists because of the UN peacekeeping operation. Without the peacekeeping presence, there would've been little or no forced prostitution in Bosnia." Lamb also pointed out that the women in the sex trade are foreigners, mostly from Romania, Moldova and Ukraine, who are brought into the region to provide services to a paying clientele, "a large component of which is foreign workers and peacekeepers."

In Bosnia, he said, trafficking and forced prostitution isn't separate from a "legitimate" prostitution trade; it's all the same. As a result, "anyone who is patronizing prostitution in Bosnia is supporting the sex slave trade. This fact is not acknowledged or disregarded by many UN peacekeepers who involve themselves with prostitution in Bosnia. Others knowingly become deeply involved in the sex slave trade, in partnership with organized crime."

Lamb informed the hushed committee chamber that organized crime warlords control the prostitution and trafficking trade in Bosnia, "most of whom came to power as aggressive and ruthless military or militia commanders during the war." These organizations, he said, are "the dominant power in Bosnia, controlling and infiltrating the political and criminal justice systems at all levels."

Lamb openly criticized the UN mission: "The UN peacekeeping operation has been ineffective at confronting the organized crime problem in Bosnia, and the Bosnian criminal justice system is still not functional to the level necessary to confront the problem." The UN, he added, has been largely passive and slow to exercise its authority. "Instead, the UN tends to practice a policy of 'out of sight, out of mind.'"

He then turned to the responsibility of the individual countries providing the police officers that make up the IPTF. While member governments have no direct role in running the UN mission, they do have control over the activities of their contingents, and "for this reason, the U.S. Department of State must share responsibility for the illicit activities of U.S. personnel." Yet the department "purposefully distances itself from U.S. IPTF members by hiring DynCorp as the middleman" and "makes no attempt to know anything about the activities of its IPTF officers who are serving as representatives and ambassadors of the United States."

Lamb concluded that "for the UN mission there are no greater problems" than those presented by the sex trade in Bosnia, adding that the UN's "cover-up policy" serves to "undermine all that the UN should stand for, particularly in the minds of the Bosnian people." Lamb's words echoed through the committee chambers, weighing heavily on the hearts of those who believe the UN makes a difference. "Illicit activities of UN personnel are no secret to the Bosnians and many of them deem the UN to be hypocritical and unworthy of governing them. These same people accept the UN presence because the alternative is worse, but nevertheless the UN has failed them."

THE UN'S LAISSEZ-FAIRE ATTITUDE is appalling. It needs to recognize the problem and take tough, unequivocal action. These men— these "peacekeepers"—are subjecting already victimized women to further servitude and abuse. The irony doesn't end there. The very aid workers who are mandated to provide assistance are using their paychecks to actually *purchase* other human beings. They buy these women for themselves and lock them up in their own apartments. The UN must recognize this for what it truly is: an abuse of authority. It must be made to stop.

"Zero tolerance" demands more than a quiet discharge or an occasional slap on the wrist. Sex with a trafficked woman who is being held as a sex slave against her will is nothing other than rape. Rape is a criminal offense. These men should be charged and prosecuted.

POSTSCRIPT

In January 2003, a 500-strong European Union–led police force replaced the UN's 1800-member multinational International Police Task Force. One of its first public relations moves was to announce the establishment of a team dedicated to counter-trafficking efforts. The EU force hit the ground by carrying out a number of raids on nightclubs and brothels. Madeleine Rees described the operations as a failure. "They were mostly for show and completely amateurish."

However, four months later, on May 8, the anti-trafficking unit scored a major PR coup when it hit a nightclub and hotel in the town of Prijedor owned by Milorad Milakovic and three associates. The EU police mission in Sarajevo proudly announced that it had smashed a major trafficking ring that may have involved up to 200 "traumatized and damaged victims." At the Masquerade nightclub-cum-brothel, for instance, police found six girls from Romania and Moldova locked in a room with metal bars on the windows.

According to mission spokesman Jon Oscar Solnes, "Indeed, the scope of the evidence gathered strongly indicates that here we have witnessed the most decisive blow against this appalling criminal activity yet seen in Bosnia and Herzegovina." The operation, he went on, "may arguably turn out to be the starting point for unraveling one of the biggest human trafficking rings of Europe."

STRAP ON YOUR
SIX-GUNS

With the diplomats at State unwilling to honestly confront foreign countries with the truth, the Office to Combat Trafficking has become the Office to Obscure Trafficking.
—GARY HAUGEN, PRESIDENT OF THE
INTERNATIONAL JUSTICE MISSION

FOR MORE THAN A DECADE grim-faced world leaders have rattled their sabers, threatening—even vowing—to implement firm measures to stop the ongoing sex crimes committed daily against defenseless women and girls. These crimes have continued unabated. What seemed to be missing from the equation is a no-nonsense, action-oriented sheriff—an individual, or better yet, an influential and powerful nation—to ride in and clean up the mess, convincingly and with authority.

In the late 1990s a handful of outraged members of Congress decided that the American government should take on the role of world sheriff and police countries around the world involved in sex trafficking and forced labor. Spearheaded by Congressman Christopher Smith, the October 2000 passage of the Victims of Trafficking and Violence Protection Act was heralded as a hopeful sign. The U.S. would use its power and influence to coerce complacent and complicit governments into action. The new law was to be the big stick that would spur political will among errant nations and force them to put an end to this modern-day slave trade.

On paper, the act is one very tough piece of legislation. In practice, it has turned out to be just another piece of paper.

One of the sticks this law provides for is the publication of an annual State Department report on how countries are dealing with the problem. It is meant to embarrass, to cajole and to trigger a swift, firm response. In the words of the State Department, the report serves "as a major diplomatic tool for the U.S. government" to help other governments "focus their future work on prosecution, protection, and prevention programs and policies."

Immediately after the act passed the sheriff went to work, ordering staff at 186 U.S. embassies and consulates to compile and file reports on the extent of trafficking in their respective host countries and the host governments' efforts to address the problem. Along with these country assessments, the sheriff amassed data from other U.S. government agencies, UN organizations, international human rights groups, the news media, academics and foreign governments. But the most valuable source of information came from those closest to the action—local and international humanitarian aid groups that worked on the front line.

The next step for the sheriff was critical—ranking the performance of each country and then placing them in "tiers." There are three of them. Tier One is for nations in full compliance with the "minimum standards" for tackling the problem of trafficking. Tier Two is for countries that are not yet meeting those minimum standards but are "making significant efforts" to do so. Then there is the infamous Tier Three, designating those nations that are neither fully compliant with the minimum standards nor making any significant effort to do so. The minimum standards are all about what governments *should* be doing to combat trafficking, and the act sets out specific criteria to determine whether countries are making serious and sustained efforts to eliminate the practice. The criteria include prosecution of perpetrators, protection of victims and educating the public about human trafficking.

According to the act, beginning with the 2003 report, the sheriff will be given the authority to start swinging the big stick and move in on the bad guys. In other words, those countries on Tier Three had better beware. They will be subject to tough sanctions, principally termination of nonhumanitarian, non-trade-related assistance. They will also face U.S. opposition to assistance from international financial institutions, specifically the International Monetary Fund and multilateral development banks such as the World Bank.

But there is a loophole. There's always a loophole. All or part of the sanctions may be waived by the U.S. president in order "to avoid significant adverse effects on vulnerable populations," not to mention "the national interest of the United States."

The first Trafficking in Persons (TIP) report card came out in July 2001, and it rattled a lot of cages. It relegated twenty-three countries—including Greece, Israel, Russia, Turkey, Romania, Yugoslavia and South Korea—to Tier Three for their abysmal records on dealing with trafficking. As expected, the rankings triggered a spate of diplomatic protests from those nations. Greece and South Korea fired off letters of protest. But the truly stunning announcement in the first report was the inclusion of Israel in Tier Three. No one ever expected the U.S. government to deliver such a public humiliation to its major Middle East ally. The move, therefore, was taken as a signal that the U.S. State Department was serious about the issue.

But despite the apparently respectable first effort, it was obvious to some observers that diplomatic considerations and politics were in play. Some of the more notorious nations with shameful trafficking records—including Moldova, Bulgaria, the Czech Republic, Georgia, Poland and Japan—somehow managed to land in Tier Two, thus avoiding the threat of economic sanctions.

International human rights organizations reined in any sharp criticism, however. After all, this was the State Department's first-ever attempt to assess the situation on a global scale. It was entitled to a few misjudgments and miscalculations. Critics figured that with a little tinkering, the 2002 report would correct the anomalies and inconsistencies and toss a slew of foot-dragging nations into Tier Three where they rightly belonged—and start the process of pushing governments around the world to move forcibly on freeing hundreds of thousands of women and girls from sexual bondage within their own national borders.

Human Rights Watch, as well as many other nongovernmental groups, strongly urged the State Department to include in its second annual report the role of state complicity and corruption in facilitating trafficking as well as government measures to identify, investigate and prosecute state agents involved in the trade. The organization also asked it to report on human rights protections of trafficking victims. More important, they wanted the State Department to include specifics on what concrete measures governments were taking to prosecute traffickers.

When the second annual report was released its wording was strong and inspired, but it rang hollow. U.S. Secretary of State Colin Powell stood at a podium in the department's news media briefing room and rattled off a prepared statement lauding the 2002 TIP Report—a 110-page document evaluating the past year's performance of eighty-nine countries. Declaring that this latest report "represents the resolve of the entire U.S. government to stop this appalling assault on the dignity of men, women and children," Powell noted that it "shines a much-needed light on this global problem. We use the information we collect to bolster the will of the international community to combat this unconscionable crime." Powell concluded that he hoped the findings would "galvanize action across the globe. If the world community works together, countless thousands can be spared abuse and despair, and those already victimized can be helped back to lives of dignity and freedom."

But a close read of the report revealed that few nations had little to be worried about, even if they did the bare minimum to stop the traffic. It did not correct the previous year's errors and it did not include any of the key concerns voiced by human rights groups. In fact, the State Department actually elevated a number of nations that it had blacklisted the year before: Albania, Yugoslavia, Romania and Israel were promoted to Tier Two, and South Korea pole-vaulted to Tier One. What had become patently obvious to the many human rights advocates who'd been pushing for tougher action is that geopolitics and cocktail diplomacy had superseded the rape of hundreds of thousands of young women and girls. The sheriff's big stick had been reduced to a limp pussy willow.

How State Department officials reached certain conclusions is puzzling. But one thing is obvious—they couldn't have read the Country Reports on Human Rights Practices their colleagues had produced just three months earlier in the Bureau of Democracy, Human Rights, and Labor. Those Country Reports deal, in part, with the trafficking situation in each country.

For example, the Country Report on Albania—a notorious source and transit country for huge numbers of East European women and girls trafficked to Italy, Greece, the Netherlands, France, Belgium, Germany and Britain—noted that trafficking "remained a serious problem," adding that government efforts to address the issue "have not yielded concrete results." The report also pointed out that "police corruption and involvement in trafficking was a problem." It went on to say that police "were often directly or indirectly involved" in the trade, and that because of corruption the Albanian Ministry of Public Order was largely ineffectual in its anti-trafficking measures. It also said the ministry failed to follow up on high-profile trafficking and corruption investigations and did not prosecute any police officers for corruption, adding that "local police often tip off traffickers when raids are scheduled." It concluded that police treatment of women "remained a problem," and that victims have been raped while in police custody.

Meanwhile, the 2002 TIP report on Albania trumpets that there were at least twelve convictions for trafficking women from December 2000 to October 2001. In fact, nine of the traffickers received only minimum sentences, and the other three—who fled the country—were sentenced in absentia. Moreover, all those convictions were later reduced to charges, such as promoting prostitution. The TIP report also states that "police corruption hinders anti-trafficking efforts" and that "10 percent of foreign victims trafficked through Albania reported that police were directly involved." Lastly, it notes that the government does not have a "comprehensive witness protection program" and that there are no government-sponsored prevention efforts." Yet for some inexplicable reason, bureaucrats at the U.S. State Department felt Albania should be elevated to Tier Two level. The sole reason it offers for the upgrade is that while Albania doesn't fully comply with the minimum standards for the elimination of trafficking, "it is making efforts to do so."

One of the more puzzling promotions to Tier Two is Yugoslavia. That this utterly corrupt trafficking nation was elevated can only be construed as either absolute ineptness or diplomatic stupidity. UN police officers and humanitarian aid workers in neighboring Bosnia-Herzogovina and Kosovo and vice-squad investigators with police departments throughout the European Union have compiled reams of reports showing that thousands of trafficking victims from Ukraine, Moldova, Russia, Romania and the Czech Republic are taken to Belgrade and other towns in Yugoslavia where they are systematically broken and then sold to pimps and brothel owners worldwide. Serbian gangsters are notorious for their brutality, and corruption permeates every level of government. Moreover, the March 2002 State Department Country Report points out that traffickers in Yugoslavia are rarely prosecuted and that the women found during police raids are prosecuted for prostitution and deported after serving their sentences.

Israel's upgrade from the worst-offender tier came as no surprise to human rights observers worldwide. To understand the State Department's decision you have to go back to the release of the first TIP report—whose stunning announcement that Israel was placed on Tier Three set cell phones ringing throughout the Washington diplomatic corps—and the intense backroom maneuvering that took place in the months that followed.

The 2001 TIP report accused the Israeli government of not making "significant efforts" to combat trafficking. It severely chastised the nation for "failing to undertake vigorous efforts against trafficking, especially given the occasional violent methods of traffickers and the significant numbers of women who are trafficked into the country." It also slammed the government for not working with other governments on trafficking cases, not conducting anti-trafficking campaigns or other efforts aimed at prevention, not actively encouraging victims to raise charges against traffickers and failing to provide adequate funding to Israeli nongovernmental organizations that assist victims of trafficking.

For Israel, the ranking had potentially explosive ramifications. That nation receives almost $3 billion in assistance from the U.S. each year. So it was no small consideration that under the U.S. Victims of Trafficking and Violence Protection Act signed into law by former president Bill Clinton in October 2000, any country listed on Tier Three when the 2003 TIP report is released will be subject to economic sanctions.

The ranking not only raised the prospect of future economic repercussions, but was also an extremely embarrassing diplomatic moment. Hookers in the Holy Land was the last thing anyone had expected as a hot-button issue in this troubled region of the world. Suddenly the eyes of the international community were focused on Israel in an attempt to understand what was going on, and, as we shall see, what was going on was absolutely shocking.

YOU HAVE ALREADY MET Sigal Rozen and Nomi Levenkron, two outspoken Israeli human rights activists. Their tiny, ramshackle office is a stone's throw from the busiest brothel neighborhood in Tel Aviv. The two women have fought a pitched battle for most of a decade trying to get their government to act decisively on the booming trafficking situation. They have been threatened and even accused of treason for bringing the issue before the United Nations and a U.S. Congressional Committee.

In a lengthy interview, Rozen, director of the Hotline for Migrant Workers—the nongovernmental agency that focuses on the plight of illegal foreign workers—and Levenkron, the Hotline's gutsy lawyer, detailed the chilling reality of prostitution in modern-day Israel. According to Rozen,

> Trafficking in women has been conducted in Israel with almost no interference for the last decade. No one knows the exact numbers but, according to estimates, every year there are about 2000 to 3000 women trafficked to Israel from the former Soviet Union for purposes of commercial sexual exploitation. This criminal activity brings millions of dollars a year to the pockets of the pimps. This ongoing situation cannot be defined as normal immigration but can only be regarded as a form of modern slavery.

For years, human rights and women's groups in Israel have lobbied the government to tackle the problem. Yet time and

again their entreaties have been rebuffed, officialdom preferring
to turn a blind eye to the egregious violations that trafficked
women suffer on a daily basis. Few people in positions of power
seemed the least bit interested in helping the victims. After all,
government ministers argued, there were more pressing issues
on the agenda.

The 2001 TIP report wasn't the first public humiliation on
this issue. On May 18, 2000, Amnesty International released a
blistering twenty-three-page report entitled "Human Rights
Abuses of Women Trafficked from the Commonwealth of
Independent States into Israel's Sex Industry." It accused the
government of failing to take even minimal steps to protect
these women, whom it effectively treated as criminals: "This is
so even though many of them have been subjected to human
rights abuses such as enslavement or torture, including rape and
other forms of sexual abuse by traffickers, pimps or others
involved in Israel's sex industry."

The Israeli Knesset reacted by amending the criminal code,
making it illegal to buy and sell human beings for prostitution,
but nothing much changed for trafficked women in the
Promised Land. Nor was the new law much of a deterrent to
thugs who went on importing hundreds of women and girls
from Ukraine, Russia, Moldova and Romania for forced labor
in the sex industry.

Human Rights Watch waded into the debate in early 2002,
taking Israel to task for failing to provide the women even
minimal human rights protections. "Trafficking victims feared
cooperating with law enforcement officials and had no incentive

to do so," HRW charged, adding that "state complicity and corruption also played a role in trafficking into Israel."

Then on March 18, 2002—just three months before the release of the second annual TIP report—the Hotline for Migrant Workers and the Israeli Awareness Center presented a joint report to the United Nations Commission on Human Rights on the "Activities and Actual Facts on the Trafficking in Persons for the Purpose of Prostitution in Israel." The groups pointed out that while meeting with the Israeli parliamentary investigative committee on trafficked women two weeks earlier, Justice Minister Meir Shitrit had attacked them for passing information on to the U.S. and the UN about the trafficking situation in Israel. "The United Nations is anti-Israeli in most of the cases," Shitrit angrily declared. "This is exactly as collaborating with the enemy—pass [your report] also to the Palestinians if you want."

In its lengthy, shocking presentation to the UN, the groups stressed that collaboration between the pimps and the police continues unabated, "whether this is in a passive manner by visiting the brothels as clients or in an active manner such as being involved in the trade and warning them of police raids. Most of the women are scared of making a complaint against the police."

It was yet another human rights embarrassment for Israel. But word began to trickle out that the U.S. State Department was about to raise Israel to Tier Two status in its upcoming TIP report. That rumor mill gained a lot of credibility when U.S. Ambassador Nancy Ely-Raphel—director of the State

Department's Office to Monitor and Combat Trafficking—appeared before the U.S. Congressional Committee on International Relations on April 24, 2002.

The topic on the table—"The UN and the Sex Slave Trade in Bosnia: Isolated Case or Larger Problem in the UN System?"—had nothing to do with Israel. Yet during her closing statement, Ely-Raphel suddenly interjected: "This hearing is about trafficking and the UN, but . . . I would like to say for the record the government of Israel has undertaken initiatives to eradicate trafficking."

At that moment everyone knew the fix was in. On June 5, 2002, Israel got elevated. At the press conference Ely-Raphel gushed that Israel was a "success story," and that it had aggressively pursued anti-trafficking initiatives since the first report was issued in 2001, "extensively coordinating with us on practical measures and policy strategies."

There was an uncomfortable silence in the room. It was obvious that in elevating Israel, human rights had taken a back seat to political diplomacy. True, Israel had made some changes to its criminal laws, but based on its overall performance it fell well short of dealing with the problem effectively. It did not merit a passing grade.

A week later Rozen and Levenkron responded to the State Department ranking with a measured press release. "This re-designation is primarily the result of vocal lobbying in Washington by Israeli and American Jewish interests. The central enforcement policy continues to focus on the deportation of women, thus treating them as criminals rather than as victims." They concluded that as long as the enforcement system in Israel "does not act in a definitive manner against the crime of trafficking, and as long as the State of Israel puts most of its efforts into lobbying in the United States rather than making sincere changes on the ground, this abominable phenomenon will continue to flourish in Israel uninterrupted."

As for the pimps, the authors added, they "typically purchase new women and continue to operate uninterrupted."

THE ASCENT OF ISRAEL, Albania and Yugoslavia to Tier Two, together with South Korea's leap from Tier Three to One and the maintenance of several nations with questionable trafficking records on Tier Two, meant that the gloves were now off. Sustained, angry criticism buffeted the State Department. Human rights workers wondered aloud how so many countries with truly abysmal records managed to escape a Tier Three ranking and its attendant U.S. sanctions and world condemnation. In total, eighteen countries perched high on Tier One; fifty-two landed safely in Tier Two, and only nineteen wallowed in Tier Three—with the exception of Russia and Greece, most of them insignificant to U.S. interests. Worldwide trafficking, during this time, continued to flourish.

Leading a vociferous attack against the 2002 TIP report was Gary Haugen, president of the International Justice Mission, a nongovernmental organization that actively investigates cases of sexual trafficking of children in developing countries. He charged that the Victims of Trafficking and Violence Protection Act "has turned out to be the whitewash that many feared":

[The report] has been rendered useless by the U.S. State Department's willingness to publicly grant passing grades to countries that are the worst offenders. With the diplomats at State unwilling to honestly confront foreign countries with the truth, the Office to Combat Trafficking has become the Office to Obscure Trafficking. That's bad news for vulnerable girls . . . and a missed opportunity for historic leadership.

Haugen also noted that for the second year, the very structure of the report continued to conceal the objective data that would allow an accurate assessment of a country's performance. "The end result," he said, "is to give a passing grade to the most egregious offenders and provide them with absolutely no incentive to change."

LaShawn Jefferson of Human Rights Watch agreed: "It's a shame that one can still read these reports and end up not knowing basic facts. For this report to be relevant, specificity matters. There is little evaluative information in the report."

With figures provided for only seven of the eighty-nine countries, the 2002 report is, indeed, virtually devoid of hard numbers. How can the State Department rate a nation's efforts if it makes no reference to numerical data? Crucial in determining a country's record are three factors: the number of women and children who have been victimized; the number of arrests, prosecutions and convictions for trafficking; and the number of police and government employees disciplined for complicity in sex trafficking.

Without these criteria, Haugen charged, the report "is disastrously unhelpful for those of us who are trying to work

with governments to eradicate sex trafficking. The report trivi-
alizes the importance of actually convicting the perpetrators of
these crimes by refusing to provide any objective data for the
worst-offending countries." As a result of this blatant omission,
"countries will not believe that the United States is serious
about its report or about trafficking."

Critics of the report also began to question the existence of
Tier Two, which some labeled a "safe harbor" for so many egre-
giously offending nations. Countries on Tier Two have actually
failed to meet the "minimum standards" in combating sex trafficking, but are nonetheless deemed by the State Department as
attempting to address the problem. In other words, they may
have passed a law or tossed a trafficker or two in prison. They
may have held a conference on trafficking and initiated a few
education and aftercare programs. The Tier Two ranking in
effect removes any incentive for these countries to do better. It
has no penalties, no consequences and little shame attached to
it. So why bother doing more?

Not two weeks after the release of the TIP report, Donna
Hughes, professor of women's studies at the University of
Rhode Island, appeared before the U.S. House Committee on
International Relations. She did not mince words. Hughes, one
of the leading voices in the campaign against trafficking, told
committee members that she hadn't heard a single word of
praise for the report.

> It has been called "an insult to women and children" . . .
> "a grave disappointment" . . . "a whitewash" . . . and "a

deplorable shirking of responsibility." As a tool to combat trafficking, it "falls short" . . . "serves to strengthen the complacency of the worst-offending countries" . . . and fails miserably in that it "undermines the usefulness of the new law."

I believe the universal severe criticism is the result of two major deficiencies in the report. First, the efforts to combat trafficking that a country had to make were pathetically low. [Second, it fails] because of a lack of comprehension of demand factors that create trafficking for the sex trade.

Hughes noted that at a briefing to nongovernmental organizations a week after the report's release, Ambassador Nancy Ely-Raphel said that the factor that weighed heaviest in determining tier placement was prosecution of traffickers. Yet there are countries in Tier Two, and even in Tier One, that have imprisoned few if any traffickers. And "even in countries where there are more convictions, there is little evidence that they have been sufficient to stem the tide of trafficking of thousands of victims," Hughes pointed out.

Ely-Raphel had also told the assembled NGO delegates that in its evaluation of a country's efforts to prevent and combat trafficking, the State Department assessment teams did not consider prostitution itself, nor the demand for trafficking victims.

An outraged Hughes reminded the committee that in the eighteenth- and nineteenth-century Southern U.S. agriculture economy, slaves were needed to pick cotton. "To not understand the relationship between prostitution and trafficking is like not understanding the relationship between slavery in the

Old South and the kidnapping of victims in Africa and the transatlantic shipment of them to our shores."

Of particular concern to the critics was the link between legalized prostitution in countries like Germany, the Netherlands and Australia and the trafficking of women and girls for the sex trade. But Ely-Raphel had downplayed the connection, stating at the briefing that she believes the trafficking of sex slaves to those countries is only "anecdotal." Her comment drew gasps of disbelief.

Hughes told House Committee members she believes "that view is either extremely naive or a gross lack of political will to face up to what the trafficking of women and children for the sex trade is all about."

Ironically, just two months before the release of the 2002 report, more than a hundred organizations representing hundreds of thousands of Americans and human rights advocates for women and children around the world sent a letter to Secretary of State Colin Powell urging him to remove the Netherlands and Germany from the vaunted Tier One rung and toss them onto a lower tier where they more rightly belonged. The organizations pointed out that in the preceding two years, both countries had legalized prostitution, pimping and brothels—"policies that will undoubtedly lead to an increase in the trafficking of women to those countries." Powell was reminded that as a minimum standard under U.S. law governments are required to make serious and sustained efforts to eliminate trafficking, and that one of the criteria is whether a country has adopted measures to prevent trafficking.

"Legalized prostitution, pimping and brothels severely violate this criterion," the letter said. "We know that legalizing prostitution, pimping and brothels increases prostitution and the need for more women in the sex industry."

While prostitution has been tolerated in the Netherlands for decades, the government officially legalized it in October 2000. Today, the Dutch sex industry is a $1-billion-a-year business, representing 5 percent of the nation's economy. Moreover, studies show that one year after legalization, traffickers in the Netherlands controlled more than half the women in prostitution and that very few Dutch women were in the brothels. They're stocked with women from thirty-two different countries, most trafficked in from Central and Eastern Europe.

The situation in Germany is similar, although the numbers of women trafficked into that country are staggering. Germany legalized prostitution in December 2001, stating officially that the practice is no longer seen as immoral. Of the 400,000 women thought to be involved in prostitution in that country, 75 percent are foreigners, 80 percent of whom come from Central and Eastern European countries. The estimated take from bars, clubs and brothels is $4.5 billion a year.

Human rights activists argue that legalized prostitution makes it extremely difficult to hold traffickers and pimps accountable for their activities. These criminals manage to avoid prosecution by claiming that the women consented to work as prostitutes. As a result, prosecutors generally complain that they face an uphill battle in establishing the line between voluntary and forced prostitution. But the more serious problem lies with the police, who can now simply ignore the burgeoning brothel industry.

The legalization of prostitution also sends a very negative message to other countries. Human rights groups contend that leaving Germany and the Netherlands on the Tier One rung might be interpreted as a tacit acceptance of legalized prostitution by the State Department. Even more worrisome is how the increased demand for women will be filled. It's obvious that the vast majority will come from other countries, and there is no doubt that many will be victims of trafficking.

Indeed, the recruitment of women for the sex industry in Germany and the Netherlands has begun in earnest. At a conference on trafficking women in Kyiv, Ukraine, in June 2000, a representative from the Dutch embassy explained that women outside the European Union have "working skills that could benefit the Netherlands," adding that the Dutch sex industry could be assisted by creating special work permits to all "foreign nationals to engage in prostitution." How benevolent of the Dutch government to offer young Ukrainian women a way out of abject poverty!

In their letter to Powell, those working diligently to put an end to the trafficking of women and children exhorted the U.S. government to use the TIP report "to send a clear message to the Netherlands, Germany and the entire world that we will stand firm against the trafficking of women for prostitution." Powell and his cronies at the State Department obviously decided to ignore the entreaty, and left both countries respectfully on the premier tier.

But let's take an even closer look at the top tier. Residing there is every single member of the European Union, with the exception of Greece, which rightly languishes on the bottom rung. There is something very wrong with this picture. The majority of these nations—including the United States, which doesn't rank itself—don't have much to brag about. The State Department doesn't seem to factor into the equation that these nations are inundated with trafficked women and that organized crime is squarely behind the trade. Nor does it consider that the vast majority of the men using trafficked women either at home or outside their borders are from the same well-heeled nations sitting smugly on Tier One.

The bottom line, of course, is that back-room diplomacy plays a major role in the tier placement process. Lisa Thompson of the Initiative Against Sexual Trafficking, a broad-based coalition headed by the Salvation Army, argued that if political considerations are part of the equation, "then the process is critically flawed. It's not about the situation in Kashmir or the tension between Palestine and Israel or all these myriad other important issues. [The TIP report] shouldn't be used to manipulate other political debates or international relationships. Otherwise it's a corrupt process and you might as well not bother."

WHILE THE DEBATE ROARED ON, staff in the Office to Combat Trafficking got down to preparing the "decisive" 2003 TIP report—the one in which countries still mired on the third tier will face tough U.S. economic sanctions.

At the 2002 TIP news conference, Ely-Raphel appeared to offer a glimpse into what to expect. More diplomatic maneuvering! This time, Russia seemed to be getting primed for an elevation. For two straight years it was listed in Tier Three, and rightly so. It has a monumental trafficking problem; the level of government and police corruption, complicity and indifference is stunning. Organized crime runs the trade with virtual impunity. The Russian government turns a blind eye to girls being recruited into prostitution even at the age of fourteen! Nonetheless, Ely-Raphel credited Moscow with initiating action on several fronts:

> Russia is working. Russia acknowledges it has a trafficking problem. It is providing funding for some victims' services and compensation, as well as protecting of rights. It is dealing with victims; they are not jailed any more or prosecuted for prostitution which had been going on before. And the Duma [Russia's Parliament] has requested advice and information from us to help draft a trafficking law. So that is all good news. However, they don't have a trafficking law. And there are rarely cases that are investigated. So that is why they're still on Tier Three. But they are making efforts.

Given the dire situation faced by trafficked women in Russia, elevating that country to Tier Two status would make a complete mockery of the Victims of Trafficking and Violence Protection Act.

Despite the tidal wave of criticism, U.S. State Department officials insist they are making the right moves. On June 19, 2002, Under Secretary Paula Dobriansky appeared before the U.S.

House Committee on International Relations to respond to attacks leveled at her department. Dobriansky countered that political considerations weren't a factor in assessing whether a foreign government is complying with the minimum standards to eliminate trafficking in persons. "Many of our friends and allies are on Tiers Two and Three," she insisted. "They simply do not comply with minimum standards."

In response to questions about the rationale used in ranking countries, Dobriansky explained:

> First, I have heard people say that placement of certain countries on Tier Two constitutes their receiving a "passing grade." There is no question that Tier Three placement is for the worst offenders, but being listed on Tier Two means that countries are not in full compliance. It's not a pass to be listed on Tier Two. Countries do not like to be listed on either Tier Two or Three and have challenged our findings. Moreover, countries on Tier Two do not want to run the risk of falling to Tier Three next year and face sanctions, including the possible cutoffs of nonhumanitarian aid.
>
> Second, and related to this, is the fact that honest people can disagree on the tier placements of certain countries. Congress asked that we look at the "significant effort" that a country is making. What constitutes a significant effort as defined in the act is something that people can discuss and analyze differently. No country—including our own—is doing enough as long as trafficking continues to exist. That said, progress in one country will look very different from progress in others, as circumstances are different and what can impact the situation may also be different.

No one believes that the laws of a single nation can halt the huge and lucrative trade in women, which ranks in dollar terms just behind drug smuggling and black-market weapons sales. The U.S. law with its stiff economic sanctions could have gone a long way toward sparing thousands of girls from a life of sexual slavery. But the fact remains that the trafficking situation is getting worse—far worse. And while those who should know better dance the diplomatic tango, tens of thousands of innocent young women and girls are ending up as sex slaves.

The U.S. government decided it would become the world sheriff. No one forced it to take on the role. Yet ever since it strapped on its six-guns, the actions of its senior deputies have trivialized the process by rewarding recalcitrance. The Victims of Trafficking and Violence Protection Act was an extraordinary opportunity to promote actions that could save the lives and health of many women and girls. That opportunity has been largely squandered.

10

THE SHERIFF'S
PLAYGROUND

*Here we are UN peacekeepers trying to establish law
and order and they're out there getting freebies
from girls being forced to be sex slaves.*

—JOHN RANDOLPH, UN COP WITH THE TRAFFICKING
IN PROSTITUTION INVESTIGATION UNIT IN KOSOVO

IN THE AMERICAN GOVERNMENT'S ATTEMPTS to grade and police world trafficking, understandably it does not rank itself; that would be a conflict of interest. Yet it does deserve a ranking. The U.S. faces a serious problem: each year an estimated 20,000 people are trafficked into the country, entering by air on bogus travel documents or smuggled overland through Canada and Mexico. On its home turf, however, the U.S. has made significant strides in aggressively pursuing traffickers, jailing them with hard time and assisting victims with a variety of programs. In fact, it can be considered a leader. So, based on its homeland efforts, it deserves to be a Tier One nation.

But in one particular criminal case, it made a colossal blunder—a blunder that resulted in the repeated rapes of several innocent young Ukrainian women trafficked into the sex trade in Los Angeles.

IT WAS THE KIND OF NEWS conference police forces dream of, yielding headlines across the country and congratulatory pats on the back. On May 3, 2001, a coterie of stern-faced federal law enforcement types gathered at the FBI field office in Los Angeles to announce a major human smuggling bust. At a makeshift podium, FBI agents, flanked by colleagues in the U.S. Border Patrol, the Immigration and Naturalization Service (INS) and the Department of Justice, announced they had smashed a sophisticated international ring that had funneled hundreds of "illegal aliens" from Ukraine into the United States through the Mexican border. But there was more to this story. Something the agents weren't talking about and must have been hoping, even praying, that the phalanx of journalists covering the event wouldn't clue into. They didn't.

The story line had the feel of a Hollywood movie. It all began with a chance discovery along a remote, dusty trail from Tijuana to San Diego. In late 1999 a U.S. Border Patrol officer on a routine inspection discovered a video camera. When he viewed the videotape he couldn't understand a word of what was being said. The language definitely wasn't

Spanish. The tape was turned over to headquarters and sent off for translation, and when it came back the boys on the border got quite the chuckle. It turned out the tape was of a Ukrainian couple documenting their illegal trek into the United States. The trail was put under surveillance and, shortly afterward, the Border Patrol snagged a Mexican guide smuggling five more Ukrainians into the country. The "illegal aliens" were interrogated, and based on the information they provided, an elaborate sting operation was launched on Valentine's Day, 2000.

By May of the following year, the ringleaders and their co-conspirators were rounded up in predawn raids throughout the Los Angeles area. The bust made for juicy headlines. The agents basked in the limelight. It wasn't every day they could boast about their successes. In all, eighteen people had been indicted, including the ringleader, her top aide and four members of her family.

"This investigation further underscores the global nature of crime . . . and the threats we now realize from abroad," FBI assistant director James DeSarno intoned at the press conference.

Assistant U.S. Attorney Dan Saunders then noted that "some of the aliens were young women who upon their arrival were sold into prostitution."

Now that tidbit of information certainly caught the attention of the media hounds. After all, smuggling people across the Mexican border into the U.S. was old news. This had a new and titillating twist. Sex sells, and smuggling young women from Kyiv to L.A. to work as hookers was the stuff of headlines.

But in recounting details of the sting, the investigators glossed over several significant facts. First—a murder. And not just any murder. The victim was Lyuda Petushenko, a prostitute and an enterprising madam who ran an upscale escort service out of her San Fernando Valley apartment. Second—six of the Ukrainians smuggled by the ring had been forced into prostitution. Four of them had been purchased by Petushenko, and one of them, a striking twenty-two-year-old blonde by the name of Oksana Meshkova, had been charged in the woman's death.

What the agents also didn't get into—mainly because the reporters didn't ask—was why the FBI, INS and U.S. Border Patrol held off rescuing these women *before* they were sold into prostitution and sexual slavery.

During the operation, between May and September of 2000, investigators wiretapped the phones, cell phones and fax machines of the key suspects involved. Based on the tapes, as well as key emails, they learned of six "events," each involving a separate group of Ukrainians being smuggled into the U.S. They also learned that one of these groups wasn't like the others: it was being trafficked into the L.A. sex market. Particularly troubling was the wiretaps' revelation that the young women in this group had no idea of the fate that awaited them. However, the listeners—the FBI—certainly knew. They heard the smugglers discuss the entire plan. They heard that the women were upset when they were told of their fate. And they heard the smugglers discussing how to keep the women from trying to escape.

Yet, while five separate groups of smuggled aliens were captured immediately by agents, some within minutes of setting foot on U.S. soil, the sixth group—the women—weren't rounded up until after the L.A. madam wound up dead . . . *six weeks down the road*. That was quite a delay—one that defies logic and crosses moral and ethical boundaries. For the victims, it spelled endless days, nights and weeks of sexual servitude. And throughout this period the authorities simply listened and watched . . . and quietly lay in wait.

The question is, What were they waiting for? The authorities knew the exact moment these women illegally entered the U.S. They could have arrested them then. More to the point, they knew exactly what was going to happen to them. They knew the women were distraught about being forced to become prostitutes. Once the women arrived, the FBI knew where they were being kept. They even heard a discussion that one of the women was raped. Still, they didn't move.

Was the FBI waiting for something more newsworthy to happen? Because if that was the intention, it most certainly did. Petushenko was brutally beaten and then shot to death at point-blank range in the chest, a murder that was directly linked to the smuggling ring. With a dead madam on their hands, the FBI scrambled into damage control. In the end, however, they had nothing to worry about. The trafficked women wound up as mere footnotes to the feature operation—the takedown of an international gang involved in people smuggling.

A key character in the conspiracy was Tetyana Komisaruk, portrayed in FBI documents as a gruff, nasty field general with a penchant for colorful language and uttering threats. Preoccupied with the details, she referred to the people she was smuggling as "the fools" or "merchandise." Tetyana was bent on keeping the profits in the family. Her smuggling empire on the American side included her husband, Valeriy, their two daughters and a son-in-law.

Whereas Tetyana lacked social graces, her top aide oozed charisma and confidence. The son of Jewish émigré parents, Serge Mezheritsky once ran unsuccessfully for city council in West Hollywood, an area heavily populated by Ukrainian and Russian émigrés. But he was hard to pin down. He went by a series of aliases, including Sergei Parfenov, Serge Merritt and Seryozha.

The gang also had several key associates in the Ukrainian capital of Kyiv, including the director and several employees of a travel agency called Svit Tours. According to a 113-page affidavit filed in the U.S. District Court in Los Angeles, the smuggling scheme had its roots in Svit Tours. It was a natural fit. The travel agents would recruit men and women in Kyiv, provide them with valid Mexican tourist visas and fly them to Mexico via Amsterdam. From Mexico City, the tourists were bussed either to a hotel in Tijuana or a villa in nearby Rosarita. Then they were smuggled into the U.S. by foot, car or boat. Once across the border, they were shuffled onto a bus or train for Los Angeles airport for flights to New York, Cleveland, Chicago and Detroit. U.S. authorities took 200 of these illegal aliens into custody, but the total count over a two-year period may have run as high as 2000. And with each tourist paying a hefty fee for the "Mexican Tour Package," the operation was a lucrative one.

While most of the illegal aliens were deported, a few were kept in the U.S. as witnesses. After Nina Rogozhyna was arrested for entering the U.S. illegally she explained to FBI agents how the operation worked. According to the sales pitch, the package included a Mexican tourist visa, round-trip airfare and hotel accommodations. The cost: $3150. More important, it included a direct link to the smugglers. On August 7, 2000, she and three other Ukrainians had left Kyiv for Mexico City. From there they boarded a bus to Tijuana, where they checked into the Plazas Las Glorias Hotel. Three days later a man who identified himself as Seryozha (Mezheritsky) met with them to set out the smuggling arrangements. The cost: $2500 cash. The next week the smugglers picked up the first two members of the group, and Seryozha informed Rogozhyna that the operation had been successful. Four days later she and the remaining member got into the trunk of a car. The car was pulled over for inspection on the U.S. side of the San Ysidro Port of Entry, and the entire group was arrested.

In short, FBI wiretaps and visual surveillance uncovered five individual smuggling operations such as this. The sixth, however, was in a league of its own. According to the FBI documents, six young women arrived in Mexico from Ukraine in early June 2000. Wiretap conversations between Tetyana and her cohorts clearly indicate that the women were going to be used as prostitutes. They also revealed that Mezheritsky had devised a grandiose plan to form a prostitution ring that would yield him $10,000 a day. To augment his criminal proceeds, he hoped to blackmail well-heeled Hollywood clients with secret videotapes of illicit sexual encounters with his women. But there was a minor hitch—the women had no idea they were being trafficked into prostitution.

In one captured phone conversation on July 2, 2000, Valeriy Komisaruk told his wife that he had just met with the women in Tijuana and that they were in shock when they heard what they were required to do. The couple talked about the possibility of the girls making a run for it. Tetyana coldly suggested that maybe he should "tie them up with chains." In another wiretap, Tetyana warned one of the buyers, Garik Vinitsky, a forty-one-year-old West Hollywood resident, that "this merchandise could easily run away." She stressed that she wouldn't be responsible if the girls bolted. "In their place I would run away within the first five minutes," she said.

On July 4, seventeen Ukrainians boarded Mezheritsky's thirty-six-foot boat. A short while later it docked at a marina in San Diego. Most of the occupants were whisked off to the train station for a quick ride to L.A. The six women, however, were escorted to the Travel Lodge near the harbor. Vinitsky was waiting. He selected two young women—Helena and Vika. Petushenko took the other four. Tetyana was paid $2500 in cash for each of the smuggled women.

Over the next several weeks, FBI surveillance revealed that Mezheritsky's plan was in full swing and that he was raking in the dough. On various occasions he discussed his operation with associates and friends, bragging about how much money the girls were making, how hard they were working and their sexual talents.

They even discussed where the girls were being housed. The FBI listened, but did nothing.

On other occasions, Mezheritsky, the pimp, directed associates where to pick up and deliver women. Still no response from the cops. In one wiretap conversation, he's heard talking about using one of the women to blackmail an unsuspecting client for a quarter of a million dollars. In another, he called his attorney, Alex Vankovn, asking him to arrange fake ID for one of the girls.

Vankovn responded, "She isn't twenty-one yet. One has to make papers for her . . . I'll have to talk to them to have it done." The lawyer later told Mezheritsky that "they're making the driver's license for her . . . It's phony but it looks real."

After a month the wiretaps showed the situation was beginning to unravel. The women were becoming uncooperative and difficult. But Mezheritsky wasn't about to let them walk away; as far as he was concerned, they still owed him money. Then the unexpected happened. Someone got killed.

On August 18, at 1:26 p.m., Mezheritsky got a frantic call from his lawyer, all captured on a wiretap.

"He killed your girlfriend . . . He killed your business completely!" Vankovn shouted.

"Absolutely, pal, he just totally killed my business," Mezheritsky replied.

The "he" they were referring to was Alex Gabay, a.k.a. "the Boxer," a thirty-six-year-old architect whose family emigrated from Russia when he was a teenager. Gabay had been a high school classmate of Mezheritsky and Vankovn.

When L.A. homicide detectives arrived at Petushenko's apartment, they found her bloodied, lifeless body sprawled on the floor of her bedroom. They were at a loss for leads. Their search yielded no tangible clues, just a closetful of expensive lingerie and a night table crammed with condoms. Then, a key discovery: as they started to trace incoming and outgoing calls, they stumbled across the FBI wiretap on Petushenko's phone. After that, it didn't take the cops long to piece together the events. The problem was distinguishing self-interest from the truth.

L.A. homicide detectives interrogated Mezheritsky on September 6 and he folded like a cheap card table. He admitted to being involved in smuggling aliens across the border from Mexico and fingered Tetyana as the ringleader, claiming she made all the travel arrangements with traffickers in Kyiv. Then he told the detectives about a trip to Mexico in early June where he happened upon six girls waiting to be transported across the border. Tetyana, he maintained, had told him they were "whores." But after speaking with them, Mezheritsky said, he quickly determined that they weren't prostitutes and had been tricked into coming to the U.S. to work as hookers. When he contacted Tetyana and voiced his concerns, he said she informed him that two individuals had already paid for the cost of the girls' passage and would be picking them up as soon as they arrived in San Diego.

Mezheritsky proclaimed he felt uncomfortable about bringing unwilling girls across the border to work as prostitutes and adamantly denied any involvement in the trade. It just wasn't something that fit with his moral compass, he said, adding that the smuggling incident involving these women was, in fact, the beginning of the end of his association with Tetyana. He said he broke off their business dealings because she was forcing girls to be prostitutes. Mezheritsky had no problem justifying smuggling desperate people into the land of opportunity, but he had to draw the line at sexual slavery.

When Tetyana was brought in for questioning on September 25, she offered a variation on the theme. She too admitted to smuggling, but vehemently denied involvement in any kind of prostitution or white slavery. Predictably, she claimed Mezheritsky was the mastermind behind the entire operation. Tetyana also told the detectives about Mezheritsky's plan to wire up several apartments with concealed video cameras so that he could blackmail large sums of money from clients who were sleeping with the prostitutes.

While their stories didn't jibe, one fact was clear to the L.A. cops: the girls had been trafficked unwillingly into prostitution. Olena G.—one of the original six—told detectives how Mezheritsky had conned her into leaving Ukraine by promising her a job as a model. She admitted being smuggled into the U.S. as part of a group of seventeen people on a boat manned by Tetyana's husband, Valeriy. Once they landed, Petushenko told her she'd have to work off an $8000 debt. Olena swore she didn't have the faintest idea that she was expected to work as a prostitute. Had she known that, she would never have left Ukraine. The accounts from the other five women were similar.

For his part, Vinitsky admitted to buying two of the women but complained that he wasn't pleased with his purchase because "they were not up for the task." It was evident, he said, that they weren't aware of what they'd be doing once they arrived and that working as prostitutes came as a shock. He noted that when he first met the women in the motel in San Diego, they didn't look right. They didn't have the right attitude for the work they were being brought in to do and were terribly distressed.

Next the homicide detectives zeroed in on "the Boxer." They learned that a few weeks before the murder, Mezheritsky had thrown a party for the four new Ukrainian women in his stable. Gabay was a guest and was instantly smitten by one of the women—Oksana Meshkova. He asked her to move into his L.A. loft. She jumped at the chance to get away from her demanding madam.

At the murder trial in January 2002, Ronald D. Hedding, Gabay's lawyer, portrayed his client as a knight rescuing a damsel in distress. He said Gabay saw a frightened young woman who was alone in a foreign country, didn't know the language and certainly didn't want to work as a prostitute. "Alex was trying to help her out. They met, they fell in love and she moved in with him," Hedding said. "You have a man who was trying to help a woman out. There was absolutely no reason for him to kill for her."

According to the evidence, on August 17, Gabay and Oksana went to Petushenko's apartment with the intention of finding out what had happened to Vika, one of the girls who had come over from Ukraine. The madam was in no mood to chat. After all, she was out $8000 because of Oksana's refusal to work off her debt. A heated argument ensued and the two women came to blows. Moments later, Petushenko lay dead on the floor from a single gunshot wound to the chest. Gabay maintained his innocence throughout the trial, saying that Oksana had shot the woman with his gun. Oksana testified that her boyfriend intervened in the argument and killed Petushenko. She too had been charged with murder, but prosecutors later dropped the case after she agreed to testify against her former lover. The jury found Gabay guilty of second-degree murder, and on March 9, 2002, he was sentenced to twenty-five years to life in prison.

The trial of the Komisaruk-Mezheritsky smuggling ring began in earnest on May 6, 2002. In his opening statement, assistant U.S. attorney Mark Aveis described the cash-only ring as a "full service" operation. He painted a portrait of an illegal family business with each member assigned specific tasks, from teaching the would-be immigrants how to act and dress American to coaching them on what to say to Border Patrol agents if they got caught. Aveis described Tetyana as the ringleader, responsible for overseeing the "comings and goings" of the smuggled Ukrainians. Her husband, Valeriy, "helped operate staging points in Mexico." Mezheritsky provided boats and cars for smuggling illegal aliens and "worked with Mexican guides to shepherd illegal aliens into the United States." Aveis also referred to hours of wiretapped cell phone conversations, which he likened to "a play-by-play commentary by defendants regarding their own activity."

Defense attorney Ellen Barry, who was representing Valeriy Komisaruk, pointed out to the jury that the smuggled aliens—witnesses for the prosecution—were no innocents. "They were willing to deceive whoever they had to deceive to get across the border," she said. "And when they got caught and found out what the government was willing to offer them, they were willing to do and say whatever they had to." Barry added that her client helped fulfill the dreams of Ukrainians desperate for a better life in the United States. "Their dream was so strong that they did whatever they could to get here."

Seven weeks later, after three days of deliberation, the ringleaders and their minions were found guilty. Tetyana was later sentenced to fourteen years in prison, Valeriy to twelve and a half years and Mezheritsky to seventeen and a half years. All tough sentences that send a clear message to criminals who contemplate getting into the business of people smuggling and the trafficking of women.

But what the trials never touched on was that the murder could have been prevented, as could the hardship the six young Ukrainian women had to endure for six long, torturous weeks. Had the FBI brought down the smuggling ring as soon as it learned what was going on, Petushenko would probably be alive today and the women pushed into prostitution wouldn't have to carry a nightmare with them for the rest of their lives.

It's not as if the evidence was inadequate or too weak to act on immediately. Various U.S. enforcement agents involved in the smuggling investigation admitted to understanding the facts and the events occurring right under their noses. Warning

signs were flashing all over. In one of many affidavits filed by
the FBI, special agent Hiram Prado of the U.S. Border Patrol
said that upon listening to the tapes, and based on his training
and experience over the years, he believed Tetyana and her
husband were talking about "smuggling females into the United
States to be prostitutes." He also said he believed that the girls
were being smuggled to be used as prostitutes "for Vinitsky and
others" and that Vinitsky contacted associates in Ukraine "to
lure girls" to the United States.

Translation: the women weren't willing participants in the
prostitution scheme. This, of course, is just one of many documents showing that the FBI understood fully what was unfold-
ing but did nothing to stop it until it was much too late. From
the very outset, it was evident that this was a classic case of trafficking in women for sexual exploitation. The wiretaps showed
that. Documents prepared by the various investigators stated
that unequivocally. It's also important to note that during the
same period the women were being kept under "surveillance,"
U.S. authorities scooped several Ukrainian aliens in five other
"smuggling events." The difference here is that none of them
were destined to work in prostitution because they all had rela-
tives and friends in the U.S. and had paid their full freight.

The only conclusion one can make of this—because the
FBI won't comment—is that U.S. authorities saw a potential
case of trafficking in women, and as it was a political hot-
button issue, they wanted to jump on the bandwagon. Why else
would they have waited? The victims first had to be trafficked
and then an iron-clad case had to be built. In other words,

like sacrificial lambs to slaughter, the Ukrainian women would have to be forced into prostitution and raped.

THE L.A. CASE, seriously botched as it was, is certainly not enough to relegate the U.S. to a lower tier. However, the U.S. must also be judged on what its ambassadors of goodwill do in foreign countries, and on this point alone it deserves to be hung on Tier Three. For one, its male citizens make up a majority of the sex tourists traveling the globe in search of one-night stands. As well, a number of notable international situations palpably demonstrate that the Americans don't practice what they preach, and that when they get caught, they retreat into crass geopolitics.

When the U.S. State Department placed South Korea on Tier Three in its first TIP report, it rightly accused the Korean government of doing "little to combat this relatively new and worsening problem of trafficking in persons." Needless to say, the slap triggered a sharp rebuke from the Koreans, an important U.S. ally in the Far East. The key phrase in the U.S. assessment was that trafficking in South Korea "is relatively new and worsening." But when Korean officials laid out the root cause in precise, unequivocal language to the Americans behind closed doors, State Department officials were ordered into scramble mode to correct the error of their ways.

A year later, the Republic of Korea was vaulted to the top tier of nations in the 2002 TIP report, which stated that the country "fully complies with minimum standards for the elimination of trafficking." Just three months earlier, however, the

State Department's own Country Report on Human Rights Practices had noted that "women from Russia are trafficked to the country for sexual exploitation."

So what was really behind the State Department's 180-degree turn? Well, the answer can be found just outside the gates of some 100 U.S. military bases in South Korea, where 37,000 American troops are stationed to defend democracy and freedom. Down the road from each base is what's referred to as a camp town or, in more graphic terms, a sexual playground for American GIs. These soldiers flock by the hundreds to bars with names like America, Dallas, Hollywood, USA, Las Vegas, Double Deuce, Cowboy and New York.

The most notorious town is Tongduchon, next to Camp Casey, the largest American base and home to 13,000 GIs from the 2nd Infantry Division. Inside the nightclubs, with signs in Korean indicating "foreigners only," scantily attired Russian and Filipino hostesses vie for the attention of lonesome soldiers. Officially, the women are "guest relations officers." The soldiers jokingly refer to them as "juicy girls." In dark stalls, young men grope the women or pay a little extra to use a back room for privacy. According to the U.S. military regulations, these bars of ill repute are off limits and any soldier caught in flagrante delicto is subject to discipline. U.S. soldiers are also required to obey the laws of their host nation, and prostitution is illegal in South Korea.

The Korean government is just as culpable in this trade as the American military. When these women enter the country on so-called entertainment visas, government officials know full well where they're going and what they'll be doing. Crudely, they're simply fodder for what is euphemistically known as R and R, an activity that dates back to when the U.S. military first arrived in the country in the 1950s.

Back then, the camp town bars were teeming with destitute, desperate Korean women. But as the years passed and economic times improved, the locals opted for real jobs in plants and factories. The bars began to empty, and somehow the void had to be filled. So the club owners united under the banner of the Korean Special Tourism Association and began lobbying the government in the late 1990s to allow foreign women into the country to work as bar hostesses. As a result the ubiquitous E-6 entertainment visa was devised, and the Special Tourism Association set out on the hunt for foreign talent. It was as easy as picking up a phone and talking to someone who knew someone with connections to organized crime. In no time, two readily available targets had been tagged: Russians and Filipinas.

A report compiled by the South Korean Justice Ministry indicates that from 1999 to 2002 the number of E-6 visas issued to foreign women rose by more than 50 percent each year. In 1999 there were 2522. A year later, 4317. In 2001 the number jumped to 6980, and in the first half of 2002, 6230 visas were issued. Of that total, more than 4200 women were listed as going to work in bars, nightclubs and hotels in camp towns near the U.S. bases. In 2002 Russian women made up the majority of "entertainers" with 1813, followed by 1471 from the Philippines, 643 from Uzbekistan, 126 from China, 113 from Ukraine, 44 from Bulgaria and 34 from Kazakhstan.

The E-6 visa is an open secret. The Korean police have acknowledged publicly that it's nothing more than a cover for prostitution. Korean women's groups have documented scores of cases in which the visa holders are victims of trafficking for prostitution rings. In other words, these women are not free agents. They're bought and owned by their pimp, usually the proprietor of the bar, and they're required to work off their purchase price by servicing American soldiers.

A report entitled "A Review of Data on Trafficking in the Republic of Korea" done for the International Organization for Migration and released at its Geneva headquarters in September 2002 concluded that "the plight of trafficked women in South Korea is quite serious." It charged that young foreign women are being lured to South Korea because they're considered "essential to the survival of the military camp town businesses, which have been suffering from a declining supply of South Korean women." The study also alluded to some level of organized criminal involvement in getting the women into the country and estimated that hundreds arrive every month to be used solely in the sex industry.

The U.S. military command has long been aware of the situation. Everyone at the Pentagon knows. The military brass would have to be blind not to see the lines of ramshackle bars as they drive in and out of the camps. Yet the practice is allowed to continue. After all, boys will be boys, and in the eyes of their commanders, they deserve a little R and R.

South Korea isn't the only place where U.S. troops indulge. On another continent halfway around the world, American soldiers—along with combatants from a host of other nations—occupy their off hours in the company of sex slaves held prisoner in scores of brothels and bars in Bosnia-Herzegovina and the renegade Serb province of Kosovo. Many of the victims—mainly from Moldova, Romania, Ukraine and Bulgaria—are mere teenagers. And the soldiers know that most of these young women have been trafficked.

Over the past three years, scores of raids to free these women have been carried out all over the region by members of the UN-mandated international police force. But there is one area that these police officers tend to avoid—the U.S.-controlled sector in Kosovo. When police raid a brothel in that sector, they do so only with the express agreement of the U.S. military command.

In October 2001, while researching the trafficking issues, I headed for Pristina, the capital of Kosovo. There I met a team of dedicated police officers in the Trafficking in Prostitution Investigation Unit (TPIU) and got the green light to take part in a series of five brothel raids. The raids would take place in the American sector. What happened shook me to my very core and opened my eyes to what was really going on.

JOHN RANDOLPH AMBLED THROUGH the crowded corridor of the courthouse in Pristina with all the confidence and bearing of a U.S. marshal. He looked impressive dressed in a royal blue jumpsuit uniform adorned with the American flag and various other badges. Randolph stands over six feet, and has dark brown hair and intense eyes. Originally a Texas lawman from Houston, he signed up with DynCorp, the American firm that recruits U.S. police officers to serve as international cops for the United Nations in various world hot spots. Randolph's mission was to bring law and order to the chaos of Kosovo. Unfortunately, he pulled the short end of the straw and was assigned to the TPIU in a backwater called Gnjilane, a town he refers to as "a cesspool" because of its huge number of brothels.

On this day in early October 2001, the officer was in the courthouse ferrying three teenage girls through the so-called judicial system. The girls had been rescued the week before in a raid on a brothel in nearby Ferrazaj. "We pulled seven girls out of the Mega Bar," Randolph began in a slow drawl. "They were all forced into prostitution by the owner. We shut the place down for good and now we're trying to get the judge to listen to what the girls have to say about what happened to them. Trouble is, the judges here prefer not to believe these girls over one of their own. They prefer to think of these girls as prostitutes and nothing more."

Randolph was one focused cop and he wasn't about to let a wishy-washy judge sidetrack his case. He had put a lot of work into the Mega Bar raid and he was definitely proud of the result. Well, almost proud. Later, sitting at a café nursing a cappuccino across the street from the courthouse, Randolph went on a rant about the bleak situation in that forsaken Balkan province.

> It's lawless. The whole place is filthy corrupt. Bar owners don't give a shit about the international cops or the local cops. The judges here are lazy, indifferent, corrupt, scared or related somehow to the accused, or any combination of the above. You can't trust them for a moment.

What really pisses me off is how useless the UN is here. For every ten international cops, eight sit on their ass and get paid for doing nothing. I'm in my office with six people and I'm the only one out there busting my butt. So I told them, "If you don't want to work, go home." They just looked at me and went on doing nothing.

But there was something else eating away at Randolph—something deeper, more sinister, and I was stunned when he finally blurted it out during his account of the Mega Bar takedown.

As I'm taking these girls out, they're waving and smiling at four KFOR [UN Kosovo Force] soldiers and two international police officers. All of them American. At the police station I asked the girls if they knew the men and they all laughed. They said the police officers and soldiers had come into the bar one evening a few days earlier boasting, "We're the law. We could shut the place down," and after having a few drinks, they got freebies. They all got Texas breathalyzers.

"What's a Texas breathalyzer?"

"That's what we call a blow job in Texas. I was so disgusted and pissed off with them. Here we are UN peacekeepers trying to establish law and order and they're out there getting freebies from girls being forced to be sex slaves."

"What did you do about it?"

"Nothing yet. I'm thinking of turning them in to Internal Affairs."

The next afternoon I returned to the courthouse. The three Romanian girls pulled from the Mega Bar raid were scheduled to give their statements before a judge. Oleksander Mazur, the no-nonsense Ukrainian cop attached to the TPIU in Pristina, escorted me into a room at the far end of the building where the girls were waiting. An officious female interpreter sat quietly on a bench across from the girls. She was reading a glossy fashion magazine.

Mazur smiled warmly at the girls and asked in Ukrainian how they were holding up. They giggled nervously and shrugged their shoulders. "Look at them. They're just girls," he said, turning to me. "When we picked them up and took them to the police station, they looked like hookers of the bottom class with their cheap makeup and very short skirts."

Not one of the girls looked older than sixteen or seventeen. They were tense and their faces were etched with worry. Just a week earlier they had been sex slaves, servicing a dozen men a night. Yet on this day, aside from their pale complexions, they looked like typical high school kids in jeans, sweaters and running shoes. Two had short brown hair and the other had dark shoulder-length hair streaked with highlights. Their faces were fresh and innocent, but their eyes told a very different story. They were filled with sadness, distrust, fear and anger. There was no hint of joy or youthful exuberance. The girls appeared disoriented and clung to each other out of fear.

"I am going to find out what is going on with the judge," Mazur said, disappearing down the crowded hallway.

Turning to the interpreter, I asked, "How did the girls end up in Ferrazaj?"

She glanced up from her magazine and put the question to the girls. Each responded in a near whisper.

"They were brought from Romania to Serbia and then over the mountains by the man who purchased them. They thought they would be working as waitresses," the interpreter said with an air of detachment.

"How long have they been here?"

Pointing to the two girls with short brown hair, she replied, "They have been here four months. The other has been here three months."

"Were they beaten at the bar where they worked?"

A few words were exchanged.

"They had to do as they were told. If they refused they were beaten."

"Were the customers locals?"

"Much of the time."

"And the other times?"

"They say there were soldiers . . . many peacekeepers."

"Do they know from where?"

"American, Greek, Turkish, Russian," the girls said. There was no need for translation.

"And international police?"

"American, Turkish, Indian, African," they said.

"Did the police officers pay them?"

The question was translated. The girls shook their heads no.

"Did any of them ever ask any of the international police officers for help?"

"No," they replied in unison.

"Why not?"

"They did not trust them."

At that moment, Mazur rushed in. "Come with me. John needs to speak with you."

Randolph looked angry as he barreled toward me.

"I spoke with my boss at DynCorp last night and he told me to stay the fuck away from you. I'm not to talk to any journalists."

"Why?" I asked.

"DynCorp hates the media!" he shouted. "My boss told me not to talk to you and he told me you're not to go on any raids."

"I have permission from UNMIK [United Nations Mission in Kosovo] to go on a raid," I said calmly.

"Not if DynCorp has any say in it," Randolph shot back.

Mazur pulled me aside. "Not to worry," he said. "DynCorp is not my boss. You will go on the raids and if John wants to stay in the office, he can stay in the office."

On October 4, 2001, Derek Chappell, a Canadian cop from Ottawa, and Romea Ponza, an Italian police officer, got the okay from UNMIK headquarters to take me on an operation targeting five brothels in Ferrazaj. Chappell explained that the raids were being kept top secret. No one on the raiding parties would be told the locations until moments before the teams were to head out. All cell phones were to be turned off during the briefing, and remain off. That way, no one could tip off a bar owner about what was about to happen. We were to rendezvous with Mazur and his team at the briefing site—the Ukrainian UN army base just outside Gnjilane—at 2200 hours. Ukrainian commandos and an elite Ukrainian canine team were to spearhead the initial takedowns. Once the bars were secured, we would go in.

That evening, Chappell, Ponza and I headed out by jeep toward Ferrazaj in the direction of the Macedonian border. The drive along a winding, pockmarked road took about two hours, crossing through three military checkpoints—one British, one Greek and one American. When we finally rolled up to the Ukrainian military base, all was dark and eerily quiet. A lone sentry guarding the main gate let us into the compound, where we met the officer in charge. He gave us the bad news.

"I was informed by Oleksander Mazur a short while ago that the operation was canceled," he said.

At Chappell's request, the officer called Mazur and handed me the phone.

"I don't know what has happened," Mazur said. "Everything was fine one minute and all of a sudden the Americans cancel the raids. Something is very wrong here. I am very much pissed off. I feel I have lost face with you."

"Did you speak to John Randolph?" I asked.

"Yes. He knew about the raids being canceled before I called him. Like I said, it is all very strange."

Mazur then said that earlier in the day, a young Romanian woman had escaped from a bar in Ferrazaj and managed to make it to Pristina. "She jumped from a third-floor window. Her name was Tina. She told the TPIU investigator here that two other Romanian girls are being held at the bar. It was one of the bars we were going to hit tonight. I feel very bad about this."

I asked Mazur for Randoph's cell phone number. He obliged.

Randolph was at a bar in Gnjilane when I reached him.

"What happened?" I asked, trying to keep my cool.

"I don't want to talk about it over the phone."

"Then I'll go where you are."

The bar was on a water-soaked, potholed road on the edge of the town. When we pulled up, Randolph was standing outside a nondescript building with a middle-aged man and woman. He was out of uniform, dressed in black jeans, a black leather jacket and a black T-shirt. The couple beside him was American and, judging from their girth, I guessed that they worked in administration. As they retreated toward the door, I noticed the sign on the window: DynCorp.

"What the hell is going on?" I asked Randolph.

"The raids were called off," he said matter-of-factly. From his demeanor, I knew he'd been into the sauce.

"Who called off the raids?"

"The commander of the American peacekeeping forces in the region," he replied gruffly.

At the door to the DynCorp office, the stout man turned to the woman and muttered loudly, "He should keep his mouth shut."

Chappell interrupted. He was heading back to the Ukrainian military compound to see what more he could find out about the decision to abort raids.

As he drove off, I turned to Randolph and asked once again, "Why were the raids called off?"

"Like I told you, the regional commander shut it down because he wasn't informed in advance by TPIU. Proper protocol wasn't followed and apparently he was pissed off."

"Protocol!" I said. "This was supposed to be a secret undercover operation from what I was led to believe. It's also a police operation against brothels holding trafficked girls, so I don't see what it has to do with the American army."

Randolph didn't respond.

"How did the American commander find out about the raids?" I asked.

"I don't know. Ask him yourself."

I kept pressing. "Did you tell anyone about the raids?"

"I told my boss."

"Which boss?"

"My boss here at DynCorp."

"You've got to be joking. You told a company that supplies U.S. cops to Kosovo about a secret UN undercover police operation! What business does an American hire-a-cop outfit have meddling in a UN operation?"

Randolph was becoming visibly agitated.

"You work for the United Nations and the operations you undertake are for the United Nations," I continued. "From where I stand, this is none of DynCorp's business."

"I work for DynCorp and the U.S. State Department. They're my bosses and if they tell me I can't take part in an operation then I don't take part. They pay my salary. They hired me and they can fire my ass tomorrow and send me home."

"I can't believe you disclosed a secret operation to DynCorp." I was boiling and trying to keep from losing it. "Are you aware that a Romanian girl escaped this morning from a bar in Ferrazaj?"

"Yeah. I know about it."

"Mazur told me she informed the cops in Pristina that two Romanian girls are being held captive in that bar. Don't you think they should be rescued?"

Randolph didn't respond, but his troubled expression spoke volumes. He looked down the road. Chappell and Ponza were approaching in the jeep.

"What was the name of that bar again? Mazur mentioned it to me," I said, knowing he hadn't.

"The Playboy," Randolph muttered.

"I gather it was one of the bars that was going to be hit tonight?"

"Yeah."

"So what are you going to do?"

"Why don't you mind your own business!" the Texan said in exasperation.

I kept up the pressure. "Do you have any idea how bad this looks? You're a UN cop and you're aware that two foreign girls are being held in a brothel against their will. You've known that since late this morning, and you're sitting in a bar drinking while they're being raped!"

"I'll get around to it."

"When?"

"I don't report to you."

"Yeah. I know. You report to DynCorp! You're pathetic."

Randolph lunged forward, his contorted face right in mine. "Get the fuck out of here." With that, he turned and stormed into the DynCorp office.

When I got to the jeep, Chappell was staring at me in disbelief.

"I thought the two of you were about to come to blows," he said. "Did he tell you why the raids were aborted?"

"No. But I have a distinct feeling it has something to do with my presence here. Probably the boys at DynCorp and the U.S. regional commander didn't want me to see any of their men being pulled out of the bars. That certainly wouldn't have been a good public relations move."

"You might be right," Chappell admitted.

In silence, we started back in the direction of Pristina. We had just passed the first military checkpoint when Chappell asked what Randolph and I were arguing about.

I recounted the story of the Romanian girl's escape earlier that day. "I was telling him how it would look that two other Romanian girls are being held captive at the same brothel while he sat at a bar drinking."

"What did he say?"

"He'll get around to it."

"Did he tell you the name of the bar?"

"Yeah, the Playboy."

Chappell stared hard at the road for a moment and then glanced over at me. We had the same thought. He made a sharp U-turn and headed for Ferrazaj. As we neared the town, a massive incandescent yellow glow bounced off the night sky. It was the lights from Camp Bondsteel—the sprawling U.S. army base. We drove into the outskirts and saw the first signs of life from a well-lit bar on the right side of the road. It was in full swing. The parking lot was jammed and rock music was blaring through the windows. The bar was called the Apache. It had been raided on several occasions, but each time the cops arrived, no girls were found on the premises. I wondered if the Apache had been on our hit list. If it was, the owner certainly had nothing to worry about on this night.

As we motored through Ferrazaj, the streets were deserted. It was a dismal, run-down, industrial town. Most of the plants and factories sat idle, rusting, caked in dust and with windows broken. Chappell made a beeline for the local police station. As we got out of the jeep he pulled out his Ottawa City Police badge and strung it around his neck along with his UNMIK identification. Chappell informed the Turkish commander of the incident involving the Romanian girl and asked if he could get some backup to check on the other two Romanians who might still be at the Playboy Club. The commander was obliging. Two international police officers—a stocky, wide-faced Bulgarian and a white-haired, raspy-voiced American—and a half-dozen Kosovar cops were assigned to lead the charge.

But moments before we were about to pull out, something unsettling occurred. As we headed toward the parking lot the American officer peeled off behind a pillar. I noticed him flip open his cell phone. When he rejoined us I asked him whom he had called. "I was calling around to see if we could get some more backup," he replied, without making eye contact.

I didn't have a good feeling in my gut.

The drive to the Playboy took less than two minutes. It was just off the main drag in a dark, narrow alley. When we marched in, the sight that awaited us was, to say the least, odd. Five young women dressed in short shorts, skimpy halters and high platform shoes were huddled together on a couch adjacent to the bar. About a dozen men sat at tables scattered around the room with their backs against the wall. It was as though they had been expecting us.

The Bulgarian officer took charge, asking the girls for their passports. One by one, they got up and dutifully retrieved them from behind the bar. Two of the women were Romanian, the other three Moldovan.

"Ask the girls if any of them is being held against their will," Chappell said.

The Bulgarian officer, who spoke Romanian, posed the question. I noticed two of the girls glance warily over at the bartender—a wiry, nasty-looking individual in a black leather jacket. All the girls shook their heads in unison. No!

"Those two definitely look afraid," I whispered to Chappell. "And they're both holding Romanian passports."

One of the girls clutched a tiny teddy bear in her right hand and averted her eyes from the police officers.

The Bulgarian turned to the bartender. "We are told two Romanian girls are being held against their will."

With a defiant sneer, the bartender countered that he didn't know what the officer was talking about.

"What's upstairs?" Chappell asked. "We're going to take a look."

Chappell and Ponza pulled out their guns and started up the concrete steps. I was right behind. On the second landing were two large rooms with four beds in each. Chappell looked down at the dressers. The cigarette butts in the ashtrays were still warm and so was the coffee in the mugs.

"Looks like they knew we were coming."

"No kidding," I said.

As we were heading back down we ran smack into an unexpected visitor—John Randolph.

"Why am I not surprised you're behind this?" he snarled as I emerged at the top of the landing.

"Well, John, I figured someone had to take the initiative to find the two Romanian girls who wanted to be rescued."

Randolph turned to Chappell. "Fancy seeing you here."

"Funny, I was just thinking the same thing."

"Did you find the two Romanian girls you're looking for?"

"The bartender says he doesn't know what we're talking about," I said.

Randolph's eyes narrowed. He instructed the white-haired cop to bring the bartender up to the second floor. A moment later he was jostling the man up the stairwell.

"Where are the two Romanian girls?" Randolph asked the bartender in a firm voice.

The Bulgarian cop translated. The bartender shrugged his shoulders.

Suddenly, Randolph grabbed the bartender by the throat and slammed him bodily into the concrete wall.

"Where are the girls?"

The bartender just sneered.

Randolph reached behind his jacket, pulled out a gun and shoved the barrel inches from the man's left eye.

"Tell me where the girls are or I'll blow your fucking head off!"

I turned to Chappell, who was shaking his head in disbelief.

"He's lost it. The guy thinks he's in a Clint Eastwood movie," I said.

"They left here two weeks ago! I took them to the Macedonian border where they took a bus back home!" the terrified bartender shouted.

"Liar! Where are they?" Randolph said, pressing the gun barrel into the man's forehead.

"They have gone. Two weeks ago. I swear!"

"We're closing this place down for good, motherfucker. You understand that? This place is history and you're going to jail for a long time if you don't tell me where those girls are."

"I do not know. They have left," he whined.

The bartender was handcuffed and dragged down the stairs.

In the bar, Randolph bellowed, "Ask these girls if they know where the two Romanians are!"

One of the girls, a skinny, hard-eyed Moldovan, spoke for the group. "They were here a week ago and they left. They went back home."

"The bartender said two weeks. She says one week. I'll bet they're both lying," I whispered to Chappell.

"We're closing the place down. We're taking the girls in for questioning," Randolph barked.

One of the girls asked the Bulgarian officer a question.

"They want to know if they can change into their regular clothes," the cop said. "They feel ashamed to be taken to the police station dressed like this."

"No," Randolph said coldly. "They're going the way they are."

But leaving wasn't going to be that easy. Outside, a large number of Kosovar men had gathered. With the bartender in handcuffs, Randolph's American sidekick pushed him forcefully toward a jeep. The locals moved in closer and the jittery Kosovar police officers retreated in the direction of the vehicles. It was beginning to look like a Mexican stand-off. The locals demanded to know why the bartender was being taken away.

"This is a police matter," the white-haired officer shouted. "This place is shut down for good. The Playboy is history!"

The Bulgarian translated, and as he spoke the locals grew bolder. They stood their ground, firing heated epithets in Albanian at the Kosovar cops, who looked worried and afraid.

On the main road, two heavily armored personnel carriers rumbled past the alleyway. They came to an abrupt halt and disgorged a dozen commandos wearing black toques and camouflage uniforms and brandishing Kalashnikov assault rifles. The sergeant was a six-foot bear of a man with steely eyes, a wide face and a square jaw. He calmly surveyed the situation. There was not a shred of fear in his face. Everyone and everything had come to a full stop as we all stared at this menacing hulk. Then I noticed the insignia over his breast pocket—a *Trysub* (Trident)—the Ukrainian symbol of freedom—and the blue-and-yellow Ukrainian flag on his shoulder.

"I'm Canadian Ukrainian," I said in my best broken Ukrainian. "How are you?"

"Dobre," he replied in a gruff voice. "What is going on here?"

"We'd like to take these girls to the police station but we've run into a bit of trouble," I said, pointing to the Albanian Kosovars.

"No problem."

He spit out a command and his men moved into position. He lowered his rifle and ordered the locals to assume the position against a wall. They were searched and told to remain in place until we left.

At the police station the girls were herded into a starkly furnished room on the second floor. They were visibly upset, cold and frightened. Randolph's attitude wasn't helping the situation. He looked pissed off and was still somewhat drunk.

"What are you going to do with them?" I asked.

"It's late," he said. "I'll process them in the morning."

"You should at least question them and see if they want out now that the bartender isn't in their face. That girl, the one holding the stuffed bear, seems really scared."

Exasperated, Randolph told the Bulgarian to escort her to a nearby office for questioning. Another officer appeared and asked the other girls if they spoke any other languages. A plump Moldovan named Maria said she spoke French. My ears perked up. I speak French. I introduced myself and asked that she accompany me to an interview room on the floor below.

Maria had been working at the Playboy for four months. Her salary was about $100 a month, and she sent the money to her parents, two younger sisters and a brother back home.

"Do your parents know what you do for a living?" I asked.

"They think I am a waitress," she said, looking at her platform shoes. "I think they know."

"Do you want to go back home?"

"To what? My family will starve to death if I don't send them this money. There is no work, no jobs in Moldova. There is only poverty."

Maria was from the town of Rocovat near the border of Ukraine. When she left Moldova she was told by a job recruiter she would be cleaning rooms at a hotel in Greece. She'd heard about the trafficking of young women, but it never occurred to her that she'd ever be recruited for the sex trade.

"I had heard about the stories of prostitution. But look at me. I am not beautiful. I am fat," she said, lifting up her blouse to reveal a roll of flesh. She didn't seem the least bit embarrassed. "I believed I would be cleaning rooms. Instead, I was taken to an apartment in Belgrade and told I was to work as a prostitute."

She said the men who held her captive in Belgrade had her stand naked for hours in front of potential buyers. No one was interested in purchasing her. Over the course of several weeks the owners fed her very little, hoping she would lose weight. They threatened that if she didn't get bought, they would sell her by the kilogram for her organs. In the end, Maria was sold for chump change and smuggled over the mountains to Ferrazaj.

I switched the topic. "What happened to the two Romanian girls?"

Maria tensed up. "They left."

"When?"

"Two days ago."

"A Romanian girl escaped from the bar earlier today. Did you know her?"

"Tina."

"She told the police in Pristina that two Romanian girls were being held at the bar."

Maria didn't respond.

"The two girls wouldn't happen to be the Romanians in the other room?"

"No. I told you, they left. I think maybe a day ago."

"It's interesting how the story of when they supposedly left keeps changing depending on who we talk to. Two weeks ago, a week, two days, a day."

Maria shrugged her shoulders and smiled meekly. She knew I knew she was lying, but there was no way she was going to come clean.

"The men who come into the bar—are they all locals?" I asked.

"No. Sometimes soldiers. Sometimes foreign police."

"Do they pay?"

"The police never pay."

"Are you sure I can't help you? I could make certain you get out of here."

Her eyes welling with tears, Maria stared down at the floor and shook her head frantically. "I cannot leave. It is too late for me. My family needs the money. Without it, they will perish."

I left Maria sitting alone with her thoughts and headed for the office upstairs. As I neared it, I could hear the Bulgarian translating for Randolph. The girls sitting in the room next door, I realized, could hear everything being said.

Randolph was sitting on a wooden chair with his feet up on the metal desk examining the girl's Romanian passport with a magnifying glass and a pair of tweezers. He was trying to determine if the document had been altered or forged. I asked if I could see it. He tossed it over. The picture was of a timid, happy nineteen-year-old named Svetlana. It had been taken two years earlier. A warm smile radiated from a round, innocent face and her eyes sparkled with the excitement of youth. A frilly blouse was buttoned up to her neck. But the young woman in the police station was no longer this person. Her eyes were hard and cynical, and when she smiled it was all part of the con. She was dressed like a cheap hooker. Her lips and fingers were painted bright cherry red. Her skirt barely covered her see-through underwear and the beige satin camisole left little to the imagination. Sitting there on a metal chair in the middle of the room, she was on display and it clearly made her uncomfortable. Her arms were wrapped tightly around her chest and she frequently pulled at her skirt in a futile attempt to hide her bare thighs.

Randolph was in preacher mode, trying to persuade the girl to change her evil ways and telling her how devastated he would be as a father to find out that this was what his teenage daughter was doing for a living. Svetlana just stared at the tiny brown teddy bear clutched in her hand.

In disbelief, I glanced over at Chappell, who looked deeply troubled.

"This is not the proper way to do this kind of interview," he whispered. "These girls should have been separated immediately and the interviews carried out in a quiet and calm manner. This girl is afraid and it's obvious she doesn't trust the police."

"With good reason," I noted.

"Do you want to go home?" the Bulgarian asked. "We can send you home."

Svetlana shrugged. She looked up at the officer, and for a fleeting moment she appeared to nod yes.

I stared at her for the longest time. The look in her dark eyes seemed to scream in pain. I was sure she was one of the girls who wanted out. My gaze shifted to the furry bear in her hand. Then I noticed a gauze bandage covering her left wrist. Along both her arms were the telltale scars of cigarette burns. Clearly, she had been tortured.

"Ask her about the injury to her wrist," I said to the Bulgarian cop.

"She said she burned herself by mistake."

"Ask about the scars on her arms. Ask if they came from cigarettes."

Svetlana pulled her arms tightly around her body and stared silently ahead.

Randolph piped up. "Do you want to go home? Yes or no!"

Again, Svetlana said nothing. She was tense and looked as though she was about to cry.

"It's late. Almost 3 a.m. and I'm tired. I'm going home," Randolph announced.

"What's going to happen to the girls?" I asked.

"I'll deal with them in the morning. I need some sleep."

When Svetlana joined the others she was greeted by icy glares. Then Ponza, the Italian police officer, showed up with a bag of clothes from the bar: sweatpants, sweaters and windbreakers. The girls jumped up and thanked her. They changed quickly, and the transformation was remarkable. They looked like ordinary young women.

I left Kosovo the next day. Chappell drove me to the Macedonian border and I headed for the airport outside Skopje. He told me he would look into the aborted raids and let me know what he found out.

AT UNMIK police headquarters in Pristina, Chappell searched for the "flash report" from the Ferrazaj police station on the Playboy raid. Surprisingly, there was none. There was no record, no mention anywhere that the raid had even taken place. When he tried to get some answers, he hit a stone wall.

A week later I phoned him from Toronto for an update. He was upset and said he was filing a complaint with Internal Affairs about the entire incident. He asked if I would do the same, and I agreed.

A few days later Chappell emailed me a copy of his complaint.

Most important, he wanted to know what happened to the women who were removed from the bar. After he'd made several inquiries, no requests were made to headquarters to assist the women. "This raid appears to have 'disappeared' officially."

I emailed Chappell my affidavit the next day, which he forwarded to Internal Affairs. He asked if I'd be willing to be interviewed by Internal Affairs. I said I had no problem with that. No one ever contacted me.

On October 21, Chappell sent me an update by email.

"I prepared a full report on the events of Oct. 4th and summarized my conclusions and suspicions. I presented the report to the Commissioner who created a special investigative team to look into all of the questions I raised," he wrote, adding that the UN police conducted raids on the Playboy and the Mega Bar that past weekend.

"We found ten women—including four at the Playboy Club from the previous week when we were there. At the Mega

Bar there was one room set up as a barracks with bunk beds around the walls where the women slept until needed for sex. No sign of Svetlana yet. Can't really say any more now."

Two weeks later, Chappell emailed another update. "I cannot find any trace of Svetlana," he began. Then he sent up a red flare.

> I get the strong feeling that there is something strange going on here regarding the internal investigation. I was interviewed several times. The last time it was a very aggressive interview in which I felt like a suspect. As a cop I feel that they are trying to shift the focus of attention from the whole issue of the aborted raid and the matter of involvement in prostitution to the single issue of John and the gun.

On December 17, 2001, I phoned Chappell. He sounded as though he'd been through the rinse cycle. "The hassles we created needed to be created," he said. "We shook things up, but having said that, the pressure is on to quiet things down. John is no longer with the prostitution unit. That is the only major accomplishment in this entire debacle. No one has been disciplined. No one has been sent home. And Svetlana is lost."

Chappell also revealed that he had met privately with an American Internal Affairs officer. The conversation left him rattled. "He's a pretty straight guy. He let it slip that 'we found something a lot worse' and then clammed up. I was told the Americans called off the raid because of a sudden request to provide protective services to local Serbs. That I know was an outright lie. When we got there, and you know that, the Ukrainian commander was with all his men waiting to move."

I managed to reach Chappell by phone on January 25, 2002. He had more intelligence to share.

> I had a very interesting conversation early this week with someone from the special investigative team. He'd had a couple of drinks and called me over for a private word. I talked to this guy for some time. He was very angry and very intense. He said a smokescreen was pulled down on the entire Internal Affairs investigation around the American K-Force and DynCorp. He said there was a lot of obstruction in the special investigation.
>
> The Internal Affairs investigator said, based on what he's been able to uncover, there was definite interference in Ferrazaj by the U.S. forces to keep the raids from going down. He felt there were Americans in those bars and that there was a lot more to this than just a few U.S. soldiers visiting brothels.
>
> As for myself, I've been asking a lot of questions and getting absolutely no cooperation. I've spoken to the head of Internal Affairs and the deputy commissioner and they won't say anything. I've asked around repeatedly about Svetlana, and since then it's like the Iron Curtain has been pulled shut around this case. I don't think we'll ever find her again.

Chappell promised to follow up with a detailed email, which he did on February 28. He'd been digging in dark recesses and gathering intelligence from a various sources, and had emerged with a disquieting lesson in geopolitics.

The U.S. Army is very tight with the Albanians, in particular the former UCK [the Albanian acronym for the Kosovo Liberation Army] fighters and their successors. The U.S. Army controls the border areas where the UCK guerillas have been trying to start a civil war with Macedonia. Most of these UCK fighters have links to organized crime. Indeed, organized crime is one of the ways that they fund the purchase of weapons.

Chappell went on to suggest that certain criminal operations in the south of Kosovo conducted by UCK fighters were being protected by the Americans in exchange for intelligence and an agreement from Kosovar fighters not to start a war with Macedonia.

"It would not surprise me if the prostitution activity is included," he wrote.

I didn't hear a word from him for several months. Then, on June 14, 2002, I called to check up on him. The conversation was terse.

"Everything has really come to a dead end," he said. "With the rotation almost all of the KFOR troops that were there last October are gone now. But the interesting thing is that the situation appears to be the same. So it doesn't seem to be something unique to that particular brigade or unit. It's almost as though that's policy, no matter who is there."

Chappell lamented that although he had tried his best to track down what he could, "there's just nowhere else to go with it. That's part of the problem when you try to do an inquiry—people rotate every six or seven or eight months."

The trail had hit quicksand.

Sadly, Chappell said he'd learned that Svetlana had been resold to a brothel somewhere in Bosnia.

GORDON MOON, the Canadian police officer who set up the first Trafficking in Prostitution Investigation Unit in Kosovo, was upset when I recounted my experience in Ferrazaj. He said that while his unit conducted raids on brothels and bars throughout the renegade province, there was one area where the bars were basically hands off—Ferrazaj and Gnjilane in the American-controlled sector.

> We felt that there were things going on there that were untoward. Now, what's obvious to me is that they [the U.S. military command] didn't want that particular crime [trafficking women into brothels] investigated because there were people there that were involved with it, that were probably receiving substantial payoffs to allow it to continue. That's why we met a pretty stiff brick wall when we were trying to establish a unit in that region.

Moon said he had ventured into the region a number of times and was appalled at what he saw. "I mean, the bars just flourished everywhere and, let me put it this way, tons of Americans in them, which kind of surprised me because the international community was supposed to be there to aid and to help people, and in turn they were fueling this prostitution and trafficking problem."

WHEN THE U.S. MILITARY effectively condones the soliciting of trafficked women overseas, it seriously undermines the efforts of the U.S. government in its anti-trafficking work. American soldiers, purportedly fighting for freedom throughout the world, are engaging in an offensive activity that represses innocent women and girls and aids criminals in making a profit. As long as this situation is allowed to continue, and as long as its citizens board planes on sex tours, the United States' ranking should be downgraded to Tier Three—with all the international embarrassment and disgrace that comes with it.

CONCLUSION:
STOP THE TRAFFIC!

OVER THE PAST DECADE the sheer scale and brutality of the sex trafficking industry has unfolded with a vengeance on the world stage. Its scope has been of such massive proportions that putting the brakes on it seems an almost impossible task. There have been conferences—endless international confabs with well-meaning human rights workers highlighting the cesspools of debauchery in different parts of the world. Social workers gather to discuss, define and document the problem. Government leaders orate with indignation and vow to put an end to the scourge. Myriad studies and research projects examine the "causes" and "effects," and enough reports have been written to fell several forests. Yet the problem persists—and has gotten infinitely worse.

An exasperated Gerard Stoudmann of the Organization for Security and Co-operation in Europe (OSCE) told delegates at

a conference in Vienna in April 2001 that European governments often provide "just lip service" on the issue and aren't
exerting enough muscle to stop it. "What is now needed," he
said, "are deeds, not words."

Mary Robinson, UN High Commissioner for Human
Rights, agrees. In a blunt speech at the Palais des Nations in
Geneva a year later, she told a hushed audience that "little has
changed for those caught up in this sordid trade. Attempts to
deal with trafficking have, thus far, been largely ineffective . . .
More people are being trafficked than ever before."

At a May 2003 conference in Noordwijk, the Netherlands,
Hamish McCullock, who heads up Interpol's human trafficking
group, pointed out that trafficking in Eastern European women
is "very much on the increase." A key factor for this, he said, is
the rise in "sexual tolerance levels" throughout Western Europe.
He also noted that better job opportunities for women from the
European Union have put a damper on the trade. Fewer and
fewer of them view prostitution as a legitimate line of work,
leaving pimps and brothel owners scrambling to find another
source. And for those at the helm of the sex industry, many of
whom are tied to organized crime, there is no easier target than
the impoverished women of Eastern Europe.

Trafficking in women is not new, nor has the world just
discovered that its women are being abducted, sold and raped.
As early as 1989 the European Parliament adopted a resolution
urgently calling for tough measures to "eradicate this practice."
In 1995, at the Fourth World Conference on Women in Beijing,
representatives from 189 countries unanimously adopted a

"Platform for Action" calling on governments around the world to "dismantle criminal networks engaged in trafficking women." And at a December 2000 world summit on organized crime in Palermo, Italy, grim-faced leaders from more than eighty countries lined up to sign the United Nations Protocol to Prevent, Suppress and Punish Trafficking in Persons, Especially Women and Children. In his closing remarks at the summit, Pino Arlacchi, then under-secretary-general of the UN, proudly proclaimed, "We all made history in Palermo." The fact that so many nations signed the protocol demonstrated "a strong and clear international commitment to achieving early ratification." Arlacchi called on countries to "ensure that the convention and its protocols enter into force within the coming twelve months."

Almost three years later, the UN Protocol—heralded as "an unprecedented instrument" that would finally provide the tools necessary for the international community to crack down on the crime—languishes in UN purgatory. Forty countries need to ratify the protocol before it's enforced, and just twenty-seven nations have done so; of these, Canada, Spain, France and Monaco are the only Western nations. Spaces for the U.S. and most of the European Union remain conspicuously blank. Ironically, ratification has come from four of the more egregious trafficking offenders—Albania, Yugoslavia, Bulgaria and Bosnia-Herzegovina—yet little has changed in these or other countries.

None of this comes as a surprise to the tiny bands of dedicated women and men working on the ground to save the victims. They know full well that, absent political will at the upper echelons of power, all the conferences, training programs, newly minted laws and wordy international protocols won't matter one bit.

Many government leaders choose instead to blame the sending countries, as if it's their fault that these "loose women" are staining their reputations. But the trade is driven by the lust of *their* men; it is fueled by the bars, brothels and bordellos dotting *their* streets; and it thrives because of *their* complacency and inaction.

In many of the sending nations, meanwhile, the attitude is "out of sight, out of mind." Local authorities argue that because the women are taken outside their borders, they have no jurisdiction or authority to act. This is a cop-out. These girls are among the most vulnerable in their society. They are the nation's daughters. They need and deserve the full protection of the state, and when they don't get it, it's a clear sign of corruption. The trafficked women are *local*. The recruiters are *local*. The women are being smuggled across *their* borders with bogus travel documents and passports. The local police see the villages and towns being emptied of young women, and they know what's behind the mass exodus. It doesn't take a rocket scientist to read a newspaper ad and see it for what it really is—a trafficking trap.

Putting a dent in this criminal enterprise requires a committed, all-out frontal assault. We need action, not just words, from political leaders, and it needs to be put into practice by prosecutors and police. We need to chase down those responsible and try them for their crimes, imposing stiff sentences that reflect the severity of what they've done. With the volumes of information now available, it's galling to watch judges sentence traffickers to mere community service. It's astounding that informed, seemingly conscientious prosecutors would negotiate plea bargains with bottom-feeding slugs. And it's disturbing that police continue to turn a blind eye to what goes on in their own backyards.

If a country is to be judged on how it deals with this scourge, that judgment must be based on the action it takes to eradicate it. The only thing that will send these thugs scurrying back into their rat holes is the full force of the law—unwavering prosecution, heavy prison time and confiscation of all profits amassed on the backs of these women. Criminals need to know that buying and selling women is not a misdemeanor and that it will not be tolerated. Not now. Not ever. And johns caught using the services of trafficked women and girls should be served notice that they too will be rounded up, charged, prosecuted and jailed.

Applying the full force of law is also the only way to get through to the corrupt cops and public officials that enable the trade to thrive. None of this could happen without them strenuously craning their necks to look the other way. Nor would police indifference be as big a problem as it is if some of the men in blue weren't slinking into the brothels and massage parlors for "freebies" on the side.

Despite the worldwide consensus on the urgent need to stop the traffic, the process is mired in endless wrangling over definitions, terminology and interpretations. Only a small number of nations have appointed a national point person or agency to coordinate anti-trafficking strategies. International cooperation on law enforcement remains sparse, and coordination even within countries is often sorely lacking. A few countries, such as the United States, have established interagency bodies to coordinate action among immigration, labor, social services and foreign affairs. Yet even there trafficking cases are frequently jammed up in bureaucratic red tape, with one department not knowing what the other is doing. The officials responsible often haven't been trained in how to identify trafficking victims, nor are immigration officers, civil servants or front-line police advised how to handle such cases. So they end up taking the easy way out by processing trafficking victims as illegal migrants and then deporting them.

And that's not the end of it. While trafficking is clearly a global problem, and while the victims and perpetrators move across borders with ease, enforcement is usually a domestic initiative subject to local policies and national laws. Not every country has enacted specific trafficking laws; and those that do exist vary from one country to the next.

Government bureaucrats lament that their nations lack an adequate legal framework to tackle the problem, with the implication that their intentions are thwarted by inadequate laws. Well, let's get one thing straight. Assault is assault. Confinement is confinement. Rape is rape. And since the sanctions for dealing with these egregious offenses already exist in law in every nation on the planet, nothing prevents them from prosecuting traffickers under their own criminal codes.

With few exceptions, most governments and police forces view trafficking in human beings as a far less serious crime than trafficking in guns or drugs. Most approach it primarily as an illegal immigration issue, and this may have something to do with unspoken biases. Better someone else's daughters, the thinking goes; at least whoever's frequenting them isn't out raping our own. Such views rear their ugly heads not only in back-room whispers but also in public debates by people who should know better. How can we ever expect to stem this odious trade if we think it's acceptable to buy, sell and rape *any* human being?

Other social biases also come into play. In the minds of most people, these women are prostitutes who have willingly chosen their route. Why should we give a damn? As heartless as it sounds, this thinking is ingrained in the minds of most cops on the beat. They steadfastly believe that virtually any woman who accepts money for sex must have entered "the world's oldest profession" with eyes wide open. They can't fathom that anyone could be so naive as to fall for the promise of "real jobs" in far-off foreign lands. As a result, the cops on the front lines rarely look beyond the mascara and the stiletto heels, and authorities seldom investigate whether the women were abducted, tricked or coerced. First and foremost, trafficking is not an illegal migration issue; it is a violation of human rights.

When a trafficking case *is* identified as such, police officers often grumble that the women aren't cooperative—that they're unwilling to talk. The fact is they are likely very afraid and distrustful, and in so many cases they have every right to be. It's hard to trust a man in a uniform when he's also a regular at the bar. Moreover, these women also know precisely what awaits them after their arrest—deportation.

And the women have been warned by their pimps about what will happen when they arrive back home if they talk. Most traffickers have local contacts. They know how to find the women and they know where their families live. Upon their return, some women have been beaten senseless. Others have been killed. For the majority, though, it is only a new beginning. According to the OSCE, "up to 50 percent of those immediately repatriated are re-trafficked."

These women would be crazy to step into the witness box without any kind of protection. Yet that is exactly what the authorities are demanding of them. Most countries have no legislation or mechanism in place to ensure their safety or fair treatment, before or after the trial. The women who decide to testify against their tormentors do so at their own peril, and once the prosecution is through with them, the file is closed. They are left to fend for themselves. It is morally wrong not to have witness protection or follow-up programs in place for trafficked women. How can we say we're serious about combating the trade if after the trial they're simply released to their captors' clutches?

From the moment they're recruited to the time they're "rescued" and deported, trafficked women are terrorized. Every single day they face a world stacked heavily against them. Their only friends are the dedicated women and men who form the thin front line against trafficking—an often thankless job. Those working for nongovernmental aid agencies and organizations are the real heroes in this bleak morass. Still, their work is merely a Band-Aid solution. In the vast majority of cases, NGO workers report that their funding is ad hoc and wholly inadequate to meet even basic needs.

If we truly want a fair shot at saving these women, we need to open not only our minds but also our wallets. We need to focus on programs that care compassionately for the victims and we need to implement them immediately, worldwide. The most urgent priorities are safe shelters and clinics equipped and staffed to offer medical and psychological treatment. We need to understand that most of these women have been psychologically and physically ripped apart. And we need to be prepared for the fact that most have been infected with various sexually transmitted diseases.

Research shows that sex trafficking is a driving force in the global spread of AIDS. Trafficked women are at an extremely high risk for infection from HIV. The very places that imprison them are breeding grounds for AIDS. Yet while the UN and world governments dole out billions of dollars on prevention and treatment, these programs do nothing to protect the millions of trafficked women and girls who are forcibly infected with the deadly virus. For AIDS prevention to be truly effective, we need to launch an all-out war against the trafficking trade. Until we do, the epidemic will continue to spread unchecked.

Another in the seemingly endless excuses for government inaction is cost. The sending countries complain they're dirt poor and unable to mount a meaningful anti-trafficking drive, while the destination nations resort to the cheapest method—deportation. In the midst of all this apathy are broken human beings. Each country where trafficked women are found should be held responsible for all the costs of protecting them and nursing them back to health. This is not a radical approach. It is the very least these nations can do to atone for the actions of its citizens—clients and pimps alike—who use and abuse these women. And there is one simple, creative and cost-effective way to fund the shelters and rescue programs: seize the proceeds and assets of the convicted pimps and brothel owners who confine these women.

Governments in the source countries must do their part in chasing down and jailing local traffickers and corrupt officials. They must also implement strong and meaningful public awareness campaigns. Young women need to be made aware of the extreme risks and dangers they face. Still, desperate people will do desperate things, and it doesn't take much to convince a destitute woman that hope awaits her in the form of a "job." We also need to address the push factor—the economic and social conditions that drive women and girls from their homelands in search of work. Until we do, traffickers will continue to find fertile recruitment fields among the impoverished women of Eastern Europe.

For the Natashas, the only avenue of escape is a real job—a serious chance at a real life. That is all they ask for, and the well-heeled nations of the West—particularly the receiving countries—have to contribute meaningfully to the solution. They must find ways of helping these women, not only with skills training but with offers of employment that don't require them to take off their clothes. The overwhelming majority of these women experience prostitution not a "job opportunity" or a "profession" but a cold hard prison sentence. The bars where they work are their torture chambers. Their bedrooms are their cells.

Clearly, no single country or institution can effectively combat this scourge alone. What we need is a firm resolve and an unequivocal commitment from around the globe to tackle this problem. Breaking this atrocious form of sexual exploitation must be a moral, legal and political imperative. One way to ensure this happens is for the world community to ratify the UN Protocol against trafficking and then enforce it with a vengeance. Trafficking of women for sexual exploitation is a crime against humanity. It shames us all. The global foot-dragging has gone on long enough. It is time to stop the traffic.

EPILOGUE

Wᴴᴀᴛ ꜱᴛᴀʀᴛᴇᴅ ᴏᴜᴛ ᴀꜱ ᴀ ᴘʀᴏᴍɪꜱɪɴɢ ꜱᴛᴇᴘ in the global fight against trafficking is now clearly a sham—an insult to the dignity of the thousands of women and girls trafficked into sexual slavery around the world. On June 11, 2003, the U.S. State Department released its third annual Trafficking in Persons report. This was to be a defining year. Countries still languishing on the dreaded third tier for their inability or unwillingness to deal with the problem would face potential withdrawal of U.S. nonhumanitarian assistance. For a handful of countries, the prospects looked grim. Russia, Turkey and Greece had landed on Tier Three for the past two years. A third Tier Three rating would be extremely embarrassing, and more than that, it would carry the threat of very real consequences. This report would show the malingerers that the U.S. meant business.

Observers were particularly wary of Russia, which has one of the worst trafficking problems in the world. Each year tens of thousands of Russian women are trafficked to more than fifty countries for sexual exploitation, and an estimated 150,000 women from the former Soviet republics work the streets and highways in and around Moscow and St. Petersburg. This monumental human rights travesty continues year in and year out for one reason—Russia, by any objective measure, is one of the most corrupt societies on the planet, not to mention home to one of the most formidable forces in the global trafficking of women: Russian Organized Crime. Russia elicited sour reviews from the U.S. State Department for the last two years in a row, and this year's review didn't sound any different:

> Russia does not currently have anti-trafficking legislation . . . Russia's legal structure still does not allow for effective prosecution of traffickers, nor for victim assistance, and efforts to prosecute traffickers for related crimes have been largely unsuccessful . . . One major obstacle to active investigations and prosecutions has been the weak legal structure related to trafficking crimes, and the small number of investigations conducted in the past year mostly failed for lack of evidence . . . Police do not respond actively to victims' complaints pursuant to the belief that any criminally proscribed behavior, such as slavery and rape, mostly happens after victims have left their jurisdiction . . . Many NGOs report corruption as a major hindrance.

Amazingly, Russia was promoted to Tier Two. The report waxes eloquent about the country's ostensible progress. It points out that the Duma, or Russian Parliament, is considering passing an anti-trafficking law and has made inroads with various public awareness campaigns. For this paltry effort, the State Department felt it was time to place Russia in the "safe zone" and, in one foul swoop, allow it to dodge a very disconcerting diplomatic dart.

John Miller, director of the Office to Monitor and Combat Trafficking in Persons, defended the promotion. "Russia had a number of general public awareness events that they hadn't had in the past year," he said. "Russia has been engaged in a Herculean effort in drafting what could well be a model anti-trafficking law . . . We're going to be looking closely at Russia and see how they perform over the coming year. We're going to look and see if this law is indeed passed, and if on the ground it is implemented."

Interestingly, Greece passed a similar law in October 2002 and yet it didn't get promoted from Tier Three. That's because, according to the 2003 TIP report, the Greek government "has not yet effectively enforced the law. Victim assistance mechanisms have not yet been implemented and NGO cooperation remains weak." Sounds an awful lot like Russia, except Russia is still just *thinking* about its law. Clearly, other factors are at play. Given their pathetic trafficking records, why else would Albania, Bulgaria, Belarus, Japan, Israel, Ukraine, Moldova and Serbia, land of the notorious breaking grounds, also get a Tier Two ranking ?

Japan managed to hang on to Tier Two for a third straight year despite the fact that it has "no national plan of action" to deal with trafficking and no law specifically prohibiting it. The number of prosecutions "has been too few and the penalties too weak to act as an effective deterrent against professional syndicates involved in trafficking." The nation also treats trafficking victims as illegal migrants and quickly deports them. It should have been demoted to Tier Three.

Israel, after receiving a Tier Three rating in the 2001 TIP report, was able to cling to Tier Two for the second year in a row. The 2003 report points out that the country's maximum penalty for trafficking is twenty years in prison, commensurate with those for rape and assault. The majority of cases, however, are resolved through plea bargains "that result, on the average, in sentences of about two years," with many sentences ranging from six months to nine years and fines. The Israeli government is investigating individual policemen for taking bribes or for tipping off brothels about imminent raids, "but these instances of corruption are not widespread."

On March 27, 2003, Israeli NGOs headed by the Hotline for Migrant Workers and the Awareness Center presented a report to the UN Commission on Human Rights. The report alleges that collaboration between traffickers and policemen

> exists in two manners: a passive manner where policemen visit the brothels as clients, and an active manner which involves cooperation with traffickers and tipping off of police raids. Out of one hundred trafficked women interviewed by the Hotline and Isha le'Isha [the Haifa Feminist Center], forty-three claimed that policemen visited the brothel as customers. Seventeen women claimed that policemen who entered the brothels officially, in order to make

passport checks, later returned as clients . . . In some cases brothels are closed just before a police raid, so the police find empty brothels. Some women complained that policemen would tip off the pimps about planned raids. Eleven women stated that the brothel owner was on friendly terms with policemen, and two women claimed to have seen money pass between them.

"When a woman is arrested by a former client," the report notes, "she is not likely to complain that she had been held in the brothel against her will."

Did the U.S. State Department even *read* this alarming document?

Another paramount issue not addressed in the 2003 TIP report is the Tier One ranking of every nation in the European Union. Every year tens of thousands of women and girls are trafficked into Austria, Germany, France, Belgium, Switzerland, the United Kingdom, Italy, Spain and the Netherlands for the burgeoning prostitution industry. Despite the now three annual State Department pronouncements that these nations are meeting the "minimum standards" for the elimination of trafficking, the situation has not improved. It has, indeed, gotten worse.

So what is the Trafficking in Persons report *really* about? The selling of women and girls into slavery every day, or projecting an image of supposed global leadership? Critics, of course, have always suspected the latter, but this latest report has confirmed the worst. The self-proclaimed sheriff who lumbered onto the world stage vowing to eradicate this scourge has finally revealed its true colors. The Trafficking in Persons report was designed to save women and girls from being sold into the flesh trade. It was supposed to be about having the courage and vision to take a firm stand. It was supposed to be about leadership. It was supposed to be about accountability. Tragically, the United States has reduced the process to nothing more than a diplomatic game.

ACKNOWLEDGMENTS

MANY PEOPLE have had a hand in writing this book and they deserve a lot of credit. First and foremost, I want to thank my family, Anna and Larissa, who have supported me on this incredibly difficult journey. Bruce Westwood, my agent, saw the urgency and power of this story and swiftly lifted it from idea to reality. Cynthia Good was a strong and passionate supporter all through the research and writing phase. Susan Folkins, my editor, has been a calm voice and a strong rudder in stormy seas, and Karen Alliston did a sensitive line edit on the manuscript.

I particularly want to thank Lesia Stangret, who has assisted me throughout this project with her diligent research, translation and critical editorial eye. I would also like to acknowledge Andrea Mozarowski for her early insights and direction; Stefko Bandera for his assistance in Kyiv; and Lorena Zuzolo for her assistance in Italy.

Along the grim trafficking trails, I met and spoke with so many dedicated people. In particular, I want to thank Madeleine Rees, Nomi Levenkron, Sigal Rozen, Leah Gruenpeter-Gold, Nissan Ben Ami, Martina Vandenberg, Don Cesare Lo Deserto, Oleksander Mazur and Derek Chappell.

I also encountered many police officers and peacekeepers who work tirelessly to stop the traffic. They are to be commended. However, it is truly unfortunate that their efforts are marred repeatedly by the actions of so many of their corrupt and amoral colleagues.

Last, and most important, my deepest appreciation goes to the many courageous young women who found the strength to share their stories.

INDEX